Indoor Plant
Gardening
for Canada

Laura Peters

LONE
PINE

Lone Pine Publishing

The Publisher: Lone Pine Publishing

10145 – 81 Avenue

Edmonton, AB, Canada T6E 1W9

Website: www.lonepinepublishing.com

1808 – B Street NW, Suite 140

Auburn, WA, USA 98001

Library and Archives Canada Cataloguing in Publication Data
Peters, Laura, 1968–
 Indoor plant gardening for Canada/ Laura Peters.

 Includes index.
 ISBN 1–55105–389–6

 1. House plants. 2. Indoor gardening. I. Title.

SB419.P39 2004   635.9'65   C2004-904008–1

Editorial Director: Nancy Foulds
Project Editor: Sandra Bit
Editorial: Shelagh Kubish, Gary Whyte, Lee Craig
Plant Styling & Photo Coordination: Laura Peters & Heather Markham
Photo Tracking: Don Williamson
Production Manager: Gene Longson
Art Direction, Book Design & Layout: Heather Markham
Production Support: Chia-Jung Chang, Ian Dawe, Lynette McKell, Elliot Engley
Cover Design: Gerry Dotto
Scanning, Separations & Film: Elite Lithographers Co.

Photography: all photos by Laura Peters, Marilyn McAra, Erika Flatt and Tamara Eder (see last page for complete listing) except: David Cavagnaro 71a & b; Derek Fell 244b; Anne Gordon 187c; Debra Knapke 187a; Tim Matheson 55; Ulrich Max Weissenberg 154 inset.

We acknowledge the financial support of the Government of Canada through the Book Publishing Industry Development Program (BPIDP) for our publishing activities.

PC: 01

Table of Contents

Acknowledgements

This book would not have become a reality without the support and love of my parents, Gary and Lucy Peters, who allowed me to follow my bliss at a very young age. Without my family, I wouldn't be doing what I love. I dedicate this book to my closest friends, who have had a question or two over the years about their houseplants. I'm sure they can guess what they're all getting for Christmas!

I would like to thank project editor Sandra Bit and book designer Heather Markham for their vision, support, hard work, enthusiasm and expertise. I would also like to thank the entire Lone Pine team, but especially Nancy Foulds, Gary Whyte and Shane Kennedy for their assistance and support. Thank you to Marilynn McAra, Erika Flatt and Tamara Eder for their beautiful images and creativity; Joseph Dougherty and Gordon Heaps for their orchid knowledge; and Ulrich Max Weissenberg for his generosity. This project would not have been possible without Salisbury Greenhouses and Landscaping, Nature's Everblooming Garden Centre, The Wellington Gift and Garden Centre and Daytona Homes Master Builder. Lastly, thank you to all who shared their love of plants with me over the years. For that, I am grateful.

About this Guide

The plants in this book are organized alphabetically by their most familiar common names, which in some cases are the proper botanical names. This enables those who are familiar only with the common name for a plant to find it easily in the book. The botanical name is always listed (in italics). Readers are strongly encouraged to learn these botanical names. Common names are sometimes spread over any number of very different plants and may also change from region to region. Only the true, botanical name for a plant defines exactly what plant it is, everywhere on the planet. Learning and using the botanical names for plants you grow allows you to discuss, research and purchase plants with supreme confidence and satisfaction.

Clearly indicated at the beginning of each entry are the main features of the plant and height, spread and sometimes length ranges, which encompass the measurements for all recommended species and varieties. At the back of the book, the Quick Reference Chart summarizes different features and requirements of the plants. You will find this chart handy when planning for plant diversity in your home.

Each entry gives clear instructions and tips for seeding, planting and growing your plants, and it recommends some of my favorite species and varieties. Keep in mind that many more hybrids, cultivars and varieties are often available than there is space

to mention. Check with your local garden centers or plant stores when making your selections. There are many plants available that are not included in this book, so I encourage you to explore. That said, I have ensured that there are plenty of wonderful plants in this book to provide you with many years of indoor gardening pleasure. Pests or diseases that commonly affect houseplants, if any, are also listed for each entry. Consult the 'Problems & Pests' section of the introduction for information on how to solve these problems.

Finally, we have kept jargon to a minimum, but check the glossary at the back of the book for any unfamiliar terms.

Introduction

Whether you consider yourself a gardener or not, growing plants indoors is a fascinating, rewarding hobby. Throughout history, plants have had a special place in our homes and workplaces. They are an inexpensive way to beautify our surroundings and provide a connection to the outdoors. And watching plants sprout and grow, flower and thrive is a great educational experience. Over the years, the popularity of indoor gardening has grown and evolved. Today, young plant enthusiasts follow trends, creating a demand for new and exotic plants over and above the tried and true.

Growing plants indoors is also healthy. Studies show that plants convert carbon dioxide to oxygen, and trap and absorb many pollutants. Many of these compounds are released into the air from everyday items in our homes and workplaces through a process called off gassing. It takes as little as one plant per 100 square feet of living area to purify and renew stale indoor air by filtering out toxins, pollutants and carbon dioxide. See list pp. 10–11.

Some people use plants as decorative accessories while others treat them as botanical specimens, collecting every species from one genus. You don't have to be a horticultural expert to derive pleasure from indoor gardening. You just need to know a little about what your plants require to grow and thrive.

Before you run out and buy a multitude of plants, it's important to know what you can and cannot grow in your environment and which plants are suited to your style and taste. This book will introduce you to a number of options, including traditional houseplants and more exotic varieties, suitable to just about any environment. Once you've chosen the right plant for the right place, you'll find out how to maintain your plants with a minimum of fuss, using the best advice and techniques available—but be prepared to experiment. You may have a few failures, but know that anyone can grow plants indoors with the right information, and this book will help with simple, concise and practical advice and solutions.

A brief history
The concept of bringing the outdoors in isn't new. Growing plants indoors has gone on for centuries, although the

status and function of indoor plants have changed over time. Whether functional or symbolic, houseplants have often been the primary element and inspiration for entire decorative schemes.

Theophrastus, an ancient Greek philosopher, is said to have started it all. He compiled a list of approximately 450 plants that were suitable for growing in enclosed spaces such as courtyards. Plants were kept under bell-shaped glass jars for exhibit as early as 500 BC. Artifacts have been discovered from Ancient Egypt proving that potted outdoor plants were grown indoors at least 4000 years ago.

Growing plants indoors didn't serve the same function then as it does today. The Egyptians often containerized formally pruned small trees in enclosed courtyards rather than rooms. The Greeks and Romans cultivated plants in a similar way because their gardens were extensions of their homes. The Chinese went even further, growing large group of containerized plants and developing the bonsai technique later perfected by the Japanese. The Arabs (Moors) practiced traditions

similar to the Romans by growing large containerized plants indoors. This practice later expanded into Europe during the Moorish occupation of Spain.

In cool climates, growing plants indoors was difficult until the advent of glass windows and heating. The first greenhouse in Europe appeared over 600 years ago; heated by an open stove, it was little more than a pavilion covered in glazed glass, but it enabled indoor gardening year-round. The motivation was to grow tender evergreens and citrus fruits. Later, the growers came to understand a plant's need for light and its intolerance to the fumes created by the open stoves.

Greenhouses as we know them today were in operation by the mid-18th century. To supply fresh stock, plant collectors were employed to search for new, exotic plant specimens in Africa, Asia and South America. As more people moved from the country to cities, their need to be surrounded by growing things became an obsession. But the open coal fires and gas and oil stoves common in most homes gave off fumes that were lethal to plants. A.A. Maconochie and Dr. Nathaniel Ward, who had created glass enclosures used to ship plants from abroad, realized that their glass cases were an ideal environment for safely growing a variety of plants, especially ferns, indoors year-round. The Victorians soon turned the glass case into a raging trend, and these cases are still used today. They are commonly known as Wardian cases or terrariums.

Since World War Two, an entire indoor plant industry has emerged as a result of the high demand for plants suited to the indoors. Botanic gardens, an integral part of the plant discovery process, trade genera and species with other gardens and collectors. Plant collection expeditions to remote destinations in jungles and deserts all over the world are still made by plant enthusiasts, collectors and nurserymen. Often, there are high expectations that the plants discovered will be successful in the indoor market. After extensive testing, many are not worthy, but every now and then a jewel is introduced to market and indoor gardeners love it.

While indoor gardening has fallen in and out of favor over the centuries, it's currently experiencing a resurgence, and for good reason. Plants provide many benefits and ask little in return.

Why have indoor plants?

The benefits to having plants in your home or workplace far outweigh the efforts required to keep them. They purify and filter the air. Some possess culinary or medicinal properties. They can soften the hard edges of any room and can make the coolest, sparsist setting seem warm and intimate.

Everyday, at work or home, we're bombarded by toxic fumes from carpets, furniture, cleaning products, printers, photocopiers and much more.

Exposure to these chemicals can result in a variety of physical symptoms sometimes referred to as 'sick building syndrome,' including dizziness, respiratory complaints and allergic reactions. If left untreated, it often leads to poor concentration and increased sick leave. Plants improve air quality by converting carbon dioxide to oxygen, and they filter and remove some of the toxins from the air. Certain plants completely remove dangerous toxins from the air over time.

After two years of intensive research, NASA has recommended a variety of plants for air purification in the average home. Similar research has discovered that common houseplants can convert chemical air pollutants into harmless substances.

The following plants have been thoroughly tested and proven to remove a variety of toxins from the air:

Alii Fig
Aloe Vera
Areca Palm
Arrowhead Vine
Azalea

Bamboo Palm
Boston Fern
Chinese Evergreen
Christmas Cactus
Chrysanthemum
Corn Plant
Croton
Cyclamen

Dendrobium Orchid
Devil's Ivy
Dumb Cane
Dwarf Banana
Dwarf Date Palm
Elephant Ear Philodendron
English Ivy
Flaming Katy
Gerbera Daisy
Heart-leaf Philodendron
Janet Craig
King of Hearts
Kimberley Queen Fern
Lacy Tree Philodendron
Lady Jane
Lady Palm
Lily Turf
Madagascar Dragon Tree
Moth Orchid
Norfolk Island Pine
Oak Leaf Ivy
Parlor Palm
Peace Lily
Peacock Plant
Poinsettia
Prayer Plant

Red Emerald Philodendron
Rubber Plant
Snake Plant
Spider Plant
Tulip
Umbrella Tree
Urn Plant
Warneckii
Wax Begonia
Weeping Fig

Plants add drama, elegance or an element of fun to any décor. Simply adding a few plants can completely transform a room. Houseplants complement a variety of interior styles, from rustic to contemporary; they add a hint of romance to a pretty room or a note of sophistication to a traditional setting. Somehow plants always seem to enhance a space and complete a room, making it a home. Plants can make even a sterile office warm and inviting. The vast array of plants available makes changing the color, structure and form of any interior easy.

Growing herbs indoors has always been popular, but now the selection of plants available for culinary, medicinal and spiritual purposes is extraordinary. Over 1000 herbs can be grown indoors during the growing season or year-round; some require light setups or a conservatory, while others are happy in a warm sunny window. There are over 40 types of basil and over 20 varieties of oregano available, for example. Your cat will even be thrilled to find catnip or cat-grass growing on the windowsill year-round.

Canadian climate

The Canadian climate, which varies greatly across the country, can be hard on outdoor plants, but indoors we can control a plant's environment. Excess humidity, one of the few climatic features that can be difficult to control, can be hard on some plants. In regions with cold winters, homes can become too dry and warm for some plants to stay healthy.

Some factors based on your regional climate must be considered when choosing indoor plants. Do you have cold winters? If so, have you put your plants next to a heat register? Can you provide humidity to compensate for winter dryness? If you live in a humid area, does excess humidity create problems for some houseplants? Are some of your plants outdoor residents during the summer months and indoor dwellers during the winter? Whatever your situation, this guide provides tips to help create the right balance of light, moisture, air and soil, the essential elements of a plant's life.

As with the outdoors, each interior space will have its own microclimates. Some places in your home or workplace will be more humid, sunnier or warmer, while others will be drier, shadier or cooler. Selecting the right plant for each microclimate is important to its success or failure. Remember, however, that you can control the environment indoors. Making adjustments is easy, fun and part of the experimentation process.

Decorating With Plants

Sometimes you can find a perfect spot for a spontaneous plant purchase, and sometimes you can't. When choosing an indoor location for a plant, there are many factors to consider. Whether your plants spend their time indoors year-round or spend the summer outdoors, it's important to consider a variety of factors, including location, prior to purchase. It's simple really: if you offer a plant what it needs, it will thrive.

Choosing the right place

Most home or workplace environments have adequate temperature, light and air quality for the average plant. However, if you want to grow a variety of plants, you will have to provide the best growing environment for each plant to ensure its success. Measures as simple as adding pebble trays, grow lights or a humidifier to a room can make the difference between survival and the trash heap.

Ask yourself these questions to determine what plant would be ideal for your space.

Is the light in the area bright, partially sunny or shaded? Light is the most important component of a plant's success. Observe the area from season to season because light levels will vary with the time of year. The "shadow test" is a simple way to deter-

the shadow test

mine the level of light. On a bright, sunny day, place a sheet of white paper in the location where you intend to put the plant. Hold your hand approximately 12" (30 cm) above the white paper to determine the definition of the shadow. The fuzzier the shadow, the lower the light. Each window will offer a different amount of light depending on its direction. We explore light in greater detail later.

Is the area you're considering an average temperature year-round? Or is it particularly hot during the winter or summer months? Or always cool or cold? Every plant grows best within a particular temperature range. If the location you have in mind never rises much above 55° F/13° C, you might want to consider a jasmine or a cyclamen, which prefer cooler conditions, rather than a bromeliad, which needs warm temperatures. Some plants prefer cooler temperatures to grow but require higher temperatures to bloom. Others require consistently warm to hot temperatures year-round to flourish. Each plant's optimum temperature preference is indicated in this book.

What percentage of humidity is in your work or home environment? Humidity is important because it plays a part in moisture loss from the plant. Plant leaves have tiny pores called stomata, through which carbon dioxide enters and oxygen and water exit. If the humidity levels are moderate to high, moisture will transpire less readily from the plant.

If you live on the prairies, then you likely experience low levels of humidity, especially in winter . Edmonton averages 86% relative humidity (RH) in the mornings and 58% in the evenings. In contrast, Vancouver exceeds 95% RH in the mornings and averages 77% in the evenings. These numbers sound ade-

quate, but remember that temperature affects humidity, especially indoors. Warm air can hold more moisture than cold air. In the winter, air enters your home at just below freezing with 50% RH, but when heated to 68° F/20° C, the RH plunges to 12%. Without supplemental moisture, the air in your home quickly becomes parched. Dry air can cause physical damage to plants, including brown leaf tips and misshapen younger leaves.

Most houseplants prefer a humidity level of about 60%. Cacti, succulents and plants native to desert environments tolerate much lower humidity (30–35%), but prefer not to drop below 20%. Plants from tropical rainforests require humidity levels of 90% or higher. Increase humidity by grouping plants together, which increases the level of moisture in the air when the

How much water does the plant need? How often and how much you water from day to day and season to season is important. Each plant has different water requirements. Once you learn more about each of your plants and get into a watering rhythm, you'll be able to judge a plant's water needs with only a brief glance.

Flowering, foliage, shape and form

The next thing to consider when choosing a plant for a particular space is overall shape. Shapes to choose from include bushy, upright, climbing/trailing, architectural and standard. These general categories give you an idea of what shape best suits the site you've chosen.

plants expel moisture through their foliage. Place plants in the bathroom or kitchen, which tend to be more humid. Use moss poles, mist regularly, double pot or use a humidifier. Terrariums or closed containers are also very effective for moisture-loving plants.

Too much humidity, which can cause fungal diseases to spread, can be reduced with a de-humidifier. High humidity occurs most often during fall, when the temperatures are cool and humidity levels are high.

Many plants fall into the bushy category, including multi-stemmed, grassy plants and single-stemmed plants covered in densely packed foliage. China doll (*Radermachera sinica*) and a multi-stemmed weeping fig (*Ficus binnendykii* 'Alii') are two good examples. Bushy plants are often rounded, dense and well clothed with foliage.

Upright plants offer structure and form. The best example of an upright plant is *Sanseveria trifasciata*, or snake plant. Upright plants display a defined, upright growth habit with no trailing or spreading. They can be small or large, and lend a vertical element to a space.

Climbing and trailing plants often have flexible stems, which trail without support or follow whatever form is provided. Philodendron is a fine example of a climbing plant. Trailing plants often cascade over the sides of the pot to form a mound of sorts. The soft stems are rarely trained to grow upwards. Trailing plants sometimes have a mat-like growth habit that clings to the sides of the pot.

Architectural plants exhibit unique and eye-catching forms in a range of shapes, textures, sizes and colors. I like to think of architectural plants as living sculpture. Typically large and displayed as specimens, they draw the eye and can stand alone. Smaller plants, such as cacti and succulents, are most effective when displayed in groups, in repetition for impact. Colored, boldly cut foliage and hairy stems are features typical of plants in the architectural category. The *Aspidistra elatior,* or cast-iron plant, has a stark but bold form that doesn't easily fall into any other category and is hard to ignore.

Standard plants are sometimes referred to as tree-like and include such plants as *Ficus benjamina,* weeping fig, or *Hibiscus rosa-sinensis,* rose of China. Some herbs are trained into a standard form to make them suitable for a formal setting. This group also includes topiary, plants that have been pruned and shaped over time to resemble small trees.

Once you have a shape in mind, the next thing to consider is whether you prefer a flowering plant or one that relies strictly on its foliage for a striking display. Some plants grown and displayed for their copious, colorful flowers bloom only for a short period. Some bloom from time to time, bearing somewhat insignificant flowers, while others don't bloom at all.

Plants available today exhibit a fantastic range of foliage colors. In addition to solid green foliage, there are variegated plants veined with gold, cream, white and yellow, and a wide array of leaf patterns, textures and colors. These marvels are best grouped with contrasting plants and decorative accessories for impact.

Choosing plants for grouping or as specimens

You now need to determine whether a group of plants would be more effective than a specimen plant for the area in question. Group plants that have the same requirements for light, water and humidity. Place taller varieties toward the back and smaller plants staggered in front or from side to side. Leave a reasonable amount of space between the pots for easy access and adequate air circulation. Plants can also be grouped together in one container, either planted directly into a larger container or left in their pots, with a little space between plants. The edge of the pots can be hidden with a

layer of moss so the arrangement appears as one.

Group plants from the same genus or family because they require the same conditions to thrive. Examples include cacti, African violets, forced bulbs and ferns. Grouping foliage plants with flowering plants effectively mixes different shades, variegations and forms. The creamy white leaf markings of a variegated plant will be highlighted by a plant with white flowers and contrasted by the solid green foliage of a third plant. Plant grouping can also be used to reinforce the color scheme of a room. Contrasting colors are emphatic and create the illusion of brightness; for example, purple foliage or flowers in a yellow room or pot can appear brighter and more colorful, simultaneously fooling and pleasing the eye. A terrarium is another means of selectively grouping tropical plants.

A specimen is an often large foliage or flowering plant displayed alone to create a dramatic effect. A specimen

plant can often provide a focal point for a special area in the home. It could be used to divide a room, to fill in a bare space or to draw the eye to a certain location, item or accessory. Placed in a conspicuous location, a small or uniquely shaped specimen can often be more effective than a towering plant out in the open. A few good examples include smaller varieties of flowering bromeliad, smaller cactus or succulent varieties and cyclamen.

Displaying plants

The last variable is how to coordinate your plant with its new surroundings. Each area of your house may be unique, or you may have a thematic design. Regardless, the climatic features will vary from room to room. Bathrooms and kitchens are often humid; living and family rooms are generally airy with natural light; and bedrooms are often sunny and warm. Every room provides an opportunity to add more plants to your collection.

An endless array of containers, pots and accessories is available for displaying plants to match any type of décor and design. Balance is a result of a plant and container that match in shape and form. Color can play into this as well. A heavily weighted, egg-shaped, granite container or round, glazed, terracotta container nicely complement a bushy, stocky plant with solid green foliage and no flowers displayed in a contemporary setting. Tall, upright plants may require a different look; try using a vase-shaped, tin bucket or a cylindrical glass or ceramic container to harmonize with the height of the plant. With flowering plants, select a container that plays on the color of the flowers so that color is part of the display even when the plant is not in bloom.

Buying Plants

When buying indoor plants, my first choice is always a reputable garden center or a retail outlet that specializes in selling plants. The plant quality and selection are usually excellent, and qualified, trained staff are available to answer all of your questions and ensure that you have everything you need to select and take care of your new plants. My second choice is local farmers' markets, which are usually stocked with indoor and outdoor plants in summer. Market vendors often grow the plants they sell, so you can rely on their knowledge and expertise. My last choice is your local big box or department store. The plants sold in these stores are usually fine when they arrive at the store, but they quickly deteriorate because of neglect and poor conditions. Because the staff aren't trained to answer questions, I would recommend a box store only for experienced indoor gardeners. Although the price will be lower than what you'd find at a garden center, you may end up with something that is diseased, insect-ridden or stressed. You get what you pay for!

You may pay more for a plant at a garden center, but you'll feel more confident knowing that you're buying a quality product, that you're armed with the best information and that you'll know where to go in the future if you have further questions.

Often the best time to buy indoor plants is from winter to mid-spring, when greenhouses are filled with houseplants. Also check stores that specialize in indoor gardening year-round.

How to check if a plant is worth buying

Be sure to examine a plant prior to purchase to ensure that it's healthy, free of insects and under no stress. The plant should be bushy, vigorous and stocky. The stems should be strong enough to support the foliage without being wobbly or spindly. Give the plant a gentle shake. If it's unstable in its pot, it may not be well rooted or may be stretched beyond a reasonable point. Any movement will also disturb insects, including whitefly, that may be hiding underneath the foliage. Avoid plants with badly damaged leaves and stems, discolored, spotted or pale foliage, brown leaf edges or tips and/or a lot of leaf loss, unless you enjoy rescuing such plants.

Check under the foliage for indications of insect infestation or damage. Look closely at the stems and soil surface for insects as well. If you see anything out of the ordinary, don't buy it. Unfortunately, if one plant is infected or infested, all the plants around it will likely be affected. Insects can travel and multiply at alarming rates and are sometimes difficult to control. Bring home a healthy, clean plant rather than a sick one that will also affect your existing plants.

Pay close attention to any flowers. If the plant is in bloom, inspect it to determine the ratio of fully open flowers to buds. A plant with a higher ratio of unopened to opened buds will have a longer blooming period. There are only two exceptions to the bud rule. When selecting a miniature rose or chrysanthemum as an indoor plant, make sure that all the flowers have begun to open. They may not open at all indoors owing to the lower light conditions in most homes.

Check under the pot. A sure sign that a plant is overdue for repotting is roots growing out of the drainage holes. Gently remove the rootball from the pot by placing the palm of your hand atop the rootball's surface, straddling the stems between your fingers for support. You may need to gently squeeze the pot or gently tap the bottom of the pot to loosen its grip. Once the rootball is loose, slowly pull it from the pot to examine it for crowded and unhealthy roots, signs of rot and pest problems. If the roots are wound

crowded, rootbound rootball vs. a newly rooted one

round the rootball like thread around a spool, then it should be repotted into a larger container. Ultimately, repotting stresses the plant and drains its reserves. Choose a plant with a less developed rootball, one with firm roots that are evenly distributed and equal in volume to the potting mix.

Roots can be different colors and sizes. They should be firm to the touch; mushy roots are a clear indication of root rot. The root tips should be slightly paler in color than the rest. Smell the rootball—you can easily determine whether rot has set in if it emits a foul smell. If it does, move on; a plant rarely recovers from root or stem rot.

Make sure you find out what you're buying. Do you know the plant's common name and its botanical name? Do you know what it will require to thrive? If the plant doesn't have a tag, or if the tag offers little information, consult the sales staff prior to taking the plant home. It's important to find out its name and care requirements before taking it home.

Protecting newly bought plants

Houseplants need to be slowly acclimatized to their new surroundings, and that includes during the trip home. The environment inside a greenhouse is dramatically different from the environment outdoors, in your car or in your home. Any exposure outdoors at any time of the year can damage or even kill your new purchase.

Wrap your new plant in paper or place it in a covered or closed box to ensure a safe trip home. Garden centers will have plant sleeves or wrap on hand for this purpose; other retailers may not. These paper sleeves are tapered at the bottom to hold the pot with enough allowance at the top to fold and seal the opening by stapling it shut. This will trap a pocket of air inside the sleeve, protecting the plant from hot sun, cool air and wind. Wrapping larger plants is sometimes more of a challenge, but it's necessary. A plastic bag tied at the top may be your only means of protection. If the plant is too large for one bag, then place the plant inside one and invert another bag over top, sealing it around the middle. It's also necessary to properly secure the plant in your vehicle to prevent it from moving around.

If temperatures outdoors are frigid, double wrap the plant for added protection. First, place the plant into a paper sleeve and seal it. If the plant is too large for a sleeve, ensure that the first layer of wrapping is paper, sealing all of the foliage inside. Then place a second layer of protective plastic over the paper cover and seal it so that warm air is trapped between the paper and the plastic. This warm pocket of air will protect the foliage from being touched by the cold air outside until you get home. Warm up your vehicle prior to placing plants in it. It only takes a minute of cold to cause irreparable damage.

Heat and wind can also irreversibly damage your plant. On a warm day,

the temperature in your car can get very hot. The inside of a vehicle on a 79° F/26° C day can reach temperatures exceeding 131°–194° F/55°–90° C, depending on the color of the interior. Rolling the windows down to cool the air can cause wind damage to the plant. Try to capture the plant's current environment at the time of transport to allow it to slowly acclimate to its new home. Try to choose the best time of day, night or season to ensure a safe voyage home. A cool evening or early morning may be better than a hot, sunny afternoon, and spring through fall may be better than winter.

Once you get your new plant home, place it in a temporary location that closely resembles the environment where you bought it. Over a period of days, move the plant into a spot where it will receive what it needs. It may show symptoms of mild shock soon after its arrival, which doesn't always indicate a problem. As it grows accustomed to its new environment, it may begin to vigorously produce new foliage and may bloom when it wasn't blooming before. It may shed a few leaves, or drop a bud or two, but over time it will gradually become used to its new surroundings if it's getting everything it requires. Don't overcompensate, just allow it to acclimatize in its own time. Within a week or two it will begin to thrive in its new home.

Growing, Maintenance & Creating the Right Environment

Plants require very little to live but can be very particular about their specific requirements. While you can't replicate each plant's native habitat, you can provide the basic elements for success. With a little compromise and careful planning, you can create the right environment to suit your plants and yourself. Although there are other needs, the four most essential components to a plant's survival are light, temperature, humidity and water, though not necessarily in that order. These basic requirements are listed with each recommended plant in the book.

Follow the basic guidelines, but you may also need to experiment with each plant. You may discover that the location you chose wasn't ideal and that you have to move the plant to another spot. Your plant may require more or less water or light than recommended, so make the necessary adjustments. Just like the outdoors, each indoor environment will have microclimates. Close observation of the area you've selected will determine if it meets your plant's needs. This is where indoor gardening differs vastly from outdoor gardening. Indoors, you have almost total control

of nearly every element of a plant's survival. Outdoors, your control is limited at best because the weather and the plant's environment can fluctuate drastically. With proper preparation, you have the power to choose what your plant receives over its lifetime.

Light, natural and artificial

Natural light is sometimes the only available or reliable source in an indoor environment. The quality and quantity of natural light changes throughout the day in every space. Only a small group of plants can tolerate direct sunlight for extended periods of time before foliage and flowers can become damaged, and this includes cacti and succulents. Some plants will tolerate or prefer shorter bursts of direct sunlight while others will only tolerate indirect or filtered light, such as through frosted glass or a sheer curtain.

Artificial light is often only supplemental, but there are situations when it may be the only source available, such as in rooms without windows and in most work environments. Incandescent light, the most common type indoors, is best for flowering plants, owing to its high proportion of red rays. Because it contains lower amounts of blue and violet rays, supplemental lighting is helpful. Incandescent light is best for plants when used in combination with fluorescent or natural light.

Some people choose to grow their plants under nothing but grow lights. The two most common forms of artificial light used primarily for growing plants are fluorescent and metal halide. Most of us are familiar with fluorescent light in public spaces, work environments and in the home. It emits a higher level of blue rays, which are best for foliage production. Although adequate for foliar plants, fluorescent light is insufficient as the sole source of light for flowering plants. Modified fluorescent lamps emit blue, violet and red rays and are often used in light tables specifically made for plant production. Metal halide lights produce an intense and complete light spectrum. The blue and white light produced by these lamps provide plants with enough light to produce foliage and flowers, but their size and expense make them impractical for home use.

Lighting is the first thing to consider when selecting a location for a plant. You need to take into account different light characteristics, such as intensity, duration and quality, as well as light availability over the span of a day and from one season to another. For example, you may have a location, brightly lit with natural light, that

Variegated and colored foliage often require higher levels of light to maintain their color.

receives two hours of direct sunlight in mid-afternoon from spring to fall, but less light daily and no direct sun in winter. Most plants do not require as much light during winter because either their growth slows down or they go dormant until spring. Either way, most plants can adapt to the ever-changing light levels found throughout the year. It is important, however, to meet a plant's light requirements year-round, especially during its active growth cycle, or the result will be a mediocre plant.

Intensity refers to the level or quantity of light. The brighter the light, the more energy the plant receives. Light can be accurately measured with a light meter in either foot-candles (imperial system) or lux (metric system) units. Intensity is often the only limiting factor when growing plants

Flaming Katy is a short-day plant.

become shorter and nights become longer. These plants form flowers only when the day length is less than about 12 hours, for example, Christmas cactus and flaming Katy. Long-day plants, such as rose of China and begonia, flower when the days become longer and nights become shorter. These bloom only when they receive more than 12 hours of light. Day-neutral plants are unaffected by duration of light and will bloom at any time regardless of day length. African violets are day neutral and will bloom any time of the year.

indoors. Variegated and colored foliage often require higher light levels to maintain their color. Intensity can be increased with supplemental lighting.

Duration, which refers to length of daylight, can affect whether a plant flowers or not. We can define three types of plants based on their flowering response to day length. A short-day plant is one that flowers when days

Light quality describes the color of light. Different rays of light affect different aspects of a plant's growth. Red light affects photosynthesis and blooming. White light is a combination of all colors and the best light for plants. A combination of natural and artificial light is best.

Although plants are happy growing in nothing but artificial light, they're often grown in supplemented natural light. The following terms describe the lighting categories that we recommend.

Bright light or **full sun** locations receive at least four to five hours of direct sunlight per day, and are often the brightest spaces in your home or work environment. Brightly lit spaces without direct sunlight also offer enough light for most plants to flower. However, not many plants can tolerate this light intensity for long periods, if at all. Most plants, even those that tolerate direct sunlight, are vulnerable to being burned by intense heat, so don't plants right next to sunny windows. Flowering plants should have no problem blooming in bright light.

Rex begonia is a long-day plant.

Moderate light locations receive bright, reflected or indirect light through the majority of the day and only a couple of hours of direct sunlight in the winter months. Only some flowering plants will bloom in these locations.

Partial shade locations have little to no direct sunlight and for shorter periods of time. With supplemental lighting, flowering plants will bloom here. Most foliage plants will do well in these locations.

Full shade locations are often poorly lit and are only favored by a small group of plants.

Direct and **indirect sunlight** refer to rays of natural light that shine directly or indirectly on the plant's location. The intensity and duration of these rays can vary from day to day, depending on weather conditions, and from season to season. Also, the sun will be higher in the sky in summer and lower in winter.

Filtered or **diffused light** has traveled through either a frosted pane of glass or through a sheer curtain. The light remains bright in most cases but is softer and less harmful to plants that are prone to burning.

Other factors may affect the intensity and quality of light indoors. White or cream-colored walls and ceilings will reflect existing light and may prevent the plant from growing toward the main light source. Well-groomed, clean foliage and clean, clear windows can increase the level of light intensity by ten percent.

Some plants benefit from being moved from one location to another based on lighting changes throughout the year. Make sure to move a plant gradually from one location to another, allowing it to properly acclimatize to different light levels. With a little experimentation, you'll soon discover where the best location is for every plant.

Temperature

Temperature is important to a plant's success. Overall, it's easy to fit plants into your home because most indoor environments that suit humans will suit plants. Also, most plants are adaptable and will survive temperatures above or below their recommended range for short periods.

It's a bit of a myth that tropical and arid plants require high temperatures to thrive. In fact, very few plants will do well in temperatures above 75° F/24° C in standard indoor conditions because the quantity of light falling on the leaves and level of moisture in the air are less indoors than outdoors in the tropics, so the need for heat is relatively less.

African violet is a day-neutral plant.

Choose the best location for each plant based on the recommended light levels and temperature ranges in this book. Generally, most indoor plants will thrive in temperatures from 55°–75° F/13°–24° C, but some plants prefer cooler or warmer temperatures. As a rule, plants prefer a drop of 5–10° F/3°–6° C at night, but a sudden drop of 20° F/11° C or more can be deadly.

A plant's native habitat determines what temperature range it prefers. Indoor plants will adapt to subtle fluctuations in temperature from day to day and season to season. Most houseplants are killed or damaged by frost or cold or freezing temperatures. If temperatures drop below the recommended minimum winter temperature, growth will slow down and may even stop. Plants may suffer irreversible damage and even die. Temperatures warmer than the recommended range may cause problems as well, but if the potting mix is kept consistently moist and the atmosphere is humid enough, most plants tolerate warmer temperatures.

a modified bottle garden

Humidity

Humidity is the one requirement that is most difficult to control indoors; it's usually too low or too high. Often, relative humidity is low in centrally heated homes, even in regions with high humidity outdoors. Central heating in winter can drastically lower humidity levels, creating very dry air.

Other than plants native to arid regions, most houseplants prefer and even require higher levels of humidity. Also, plants with thin, papery foliage usually need more moisture in the air than plants with succulent foliage. Houseplants require moist air more than they require warm air.

Some rooms in the house, such as bathrooms and kitchens, naturally have higher humidity, but you can't put every plant in those spaces.

You can easily boost humidity within a terrarium. Terrariums and bottle gardens were created for just this purpose. For plants that require a moist atmosphere, a terrarium is the ideal place. Conservatories and greenhouses are also ideal but can be too expensive and impractical.

There is only one way to reduce humidity, but there are many simple, easy and inexpensive ways to increase humidity for your plants, individually or collectively. These include misting, grouping, pebble trays, double potting and humidifiers, or even something as simple as placing humidity trays over radiators and heaters. These techniques can increase the relative humidity of dry indoor air to 30–60%, the ideal range for most indoor plants. When misting, use water at room temperature or tepid water, and mist your plants at a cooler time of day, preferably in morning so the foliage can dry before dark. Avoid misting when the plant is exposed to direct sunlight because doing so may damage the foliage. Try to cover the entire plant by depositing a fine coating of water on the stems and on both sides of each leaf. Avoid wetting buds or flowers.

Misting your plants does more than just increase humidity levels. It discourages red spider mite attacks and other insect infestations. It also reduces dust deposits on the foliage and has a cooling effect on warmer days. Misting forces you to pay closer attention to each plant, giving you an opportunity to inspect your plants for anything out of the ordinary.

Grouping plants can increase humidity levels. In a process called transpiration, moisture escapes from the surface of the foliage through the stomata or pores. This process increases water vapor in the atmosphere in the immediate vicinity of each plant, creating a humid microclimate. Moisture is also simultaneously evaporating from the saturated potting mix, further increasing humidity. Avoid placing plants too close to one another. There should be adequate space around each plant for air to freely circulate to prevent the onset of *Botrytis*, which occurs when high humidity is combined with poorly circulating air.

Pebble trays are an easy, practical and beautiful way to supplement humidity levels. This method is ideal and even crucial for individual specimens, larger plants, those not tolerant of misting or those too large for double potting. Simply place a layer of pea-sized gravel or tiny glass beads, polished stones or decorative rock in a waterproof, shallow drainage saucer, dish or tray, and then add water. Place the plant pot on top of the rock so that it sits above, not in, the water. As the water evaporates, it increases water vapor in the air around the plant.

Pebble trays often dry out faster than you can refill them, and they can get a little swampy. If the water sits for too long, it may go rancid and begin to smell, bacteria could start to proliferate and fungus may even form. If any of these things occur, dump the water out

pebble trays, mister, humidifier and a digital hygrometer

entire house. Humidifiers use little energy, take up little space and will benefit both you and your plants.

When excess humidity is a problem, the only method of reducing the level of moisture in the air is using a dehumidifier. These are relatively inexpensive and do a remarkable job. Excessive humidity can lead to problems with *Botrytis*, so it's best to maintain a healthy level of relative humidity.

Water

Water is one of the most important factors in a plant's survival, if not the most important. How much and how frequently you water determine your plants' survival. Most garden centers say: "the one who's in charge of watering has the most important job."

Watering is a simple job, but it takes a little practice to determine when and how much to water. If you're a beginner indoor gardener, a variety of useful watering techniques and products are available to help you develop a watering routine. When you become familiar with what is necessary for your plants' success, you'll be able to gauge their watering needs by their appearance and weight alone, with the occasional probe using the cheapest, most accurate and easily accessible water meter ever discovered—your finger.

The few rules to follow when watering your indoor plants are similar to the rules for watering outdoors. Each plant will require water at different times and for different reasons. A number of factors will play into watering quantity and frequency, including the size and type of pot, potting mix, type of plant, time of year, level of humidity, temperature and light. Some of these variables can change from day to day while others will remain constant.

and submerge the tray and pebbles into a solution of 10% bleach and soapy water for 15 minutes. Rinse and reassemble. Stagnant water, bacteria and fungus growth may be indications that your humidity levels are okay after all. If the water isn't evaporating quickly, monitor the percentage of relative humidity and remove the pebble trays if humidity levels are adequate or better.

Double potting is another way to supplement humidity levels. Insert the nursery pot with the plant into a larger decorative, waterproof pot filled with moist peat moss. As the moisture evaporates from the peat moss, water vapor is released into the surrounding air. Keep the peat moss continually moist. This method also acts as a regulating barrier that insulates the rootball, protecting it from sudden fluctuations in temperature.

Lastly, add a humidifier. Many humidifiers, in varying sizes and prices, are available today. A small, tabletop humidifier will increase the relative humidity in a smaller space like a bedroom, den or office. A large, portable or built-in humidifier can increase the humidity throughout the

Use a good quality, long-necked watering can, which will extend your reach and control the flow and direction of the water, preventing any of the potting mix from washing away.

Often plants are killed with kindness; they are frequently overwatered, resulting in rot and, eventually, death. When a rootball becomes waterlogged, air is no longer able to reach the roots. Remember that you can't take water away but you can always add more. Once rot has set in, the damage is done and there is no turning back, so err on the side of caution and water carefully.

First, determine if a plant needs water by lifting the pot, if it's not too large, or by sticking your finger into the first inch or so of the potting mix. Checking pot weight works well with smaller containers. The pot will be lighter if the soil is dry and heavier if it's wet. Familiarize yourself with each pot, lift to estimate how heavy it is when it's drying out and how the weight differs when it's completely saturated. Over time you will become familiar with the weight of each container. This process can be a little time consuming and labor intensive, however, and it's not the solution for every pot. The best method is to look and feel. Appearance alone can be a great guide, but it can also be a little deceiving to the beginner. The mix might be dry on the surface but moist underneath. This is where touch is most effective.

Compared to soil-based

mixes, peat moss–based or soil-less mixes appear paler when dry and can dry out more quickly, but there are advantages to both. When using peat moss–based or soil-less mixes, do not allow them to dry out beyond a certain point because it becomes difficult to wet the mixture again. The mix will shrink, coming away from the pot, and will repel water. Often plants that prefer a peat based– or soil-less mix should be kept consistently moist to prevent such shrinkage. The surface of moist peat or soil-less mix should feel soft and a little spongy, whereas dry mix will feel hard and somewhat unforgiving.

A soil-based mix will be almost black when completely saturated and a lighter shade of gray when dry. The surface of a moist soil mix should feel soft, whereas a dry soil mix will be hard but dusty.

There are two methods of watering. Most plants are simply watered from above or on the soil's surface while others prefer to be immersed into water. Some plants, including African violets and cyclamen, resent having wet foliage or flowers and will look damaged. Generally, plants with hairy foliage and plants in flower prefer the immersion method. If watering from above, time your watering carefully because wet foliage may become scorched in bright or direct sunlight.

Once you've determined that your plants require water, how do you know how much to give and

watering from above

the immersion method

rootball has dried out, however, the water may just roll off the top, down the sides and out the bottom without being absorbed. If this occurs to a plant that is normally watered from the top, place the pot in a sealed, waterproof container with at least 3–4" (7.6–10 cm) of water in the bottom (*left*). Let the pot sit in the water until the water has been drawn into the rootball as if into a sponge. This process may take a little while, but it's important to saturate the entire rootball. The rootball may float on the surface rather than absorb the water. If so, gently weigh the rootball down, completely submerging it under water until all of the air bubbles have stopped coming to the surface.

Once you have saturated the rootball, remove any standing water in the drainage tray or saucer. The only time you would allow the excess water to remain is when it drains directly into a pebble tray. There is less chance of rot as long as the pot and rootball are standing above the water and not in it. Standing water, if left long enough, can also become stagnant, smelly and ridden with bacteria.

I find that, if I recommend watering sparingly, the beginner will water the top half of a plant while leaving the bottom half dry. Watering sparingly should only be practiced when absolutely necessary, and then only by more experienced indoor gardeners who can recognize the signs that their plants are begging for water.

Accessories such as water meters, indicator strips and self-watering pots may be helpful, but are not always reliable and can even be a little deceptive. You'll also grow tired of pushing a device into every plant to determine moisture levels. It's better to educate your eye and sense of touch, two tools

when? There are no hard and fast rules, but there are some general guidelines. Most importantly, remember to water thoroughly and infrequently. Some plants need to be watered every two days, some weekly and others only monthly. When you water, make sure to thoroughly saturate the entire rootball.

If you have immersed the rootball in water, wait until the mix surface is moist, then remove the rootball from the water. When watering from above, fill the space from the mix surface to the pot's rim and wait until the water trickles from the drainage holes at the bottom, proof that the water has gone completely through the rootball. If the you can always rely on that are always available and cost nothing.

Water quality is an issue when watering plants indoors and outdoors. Filtered water is best but isn't always convenient, available or cost efficient. Rainwater is ideal but also not always available. Tap water isn't the best but is often the most common source of water for houseplants. Most plants will tolerate it, depending on hardness, which can vary from place to place. Hard water is a problem in a number of regions throughout the country. Boiling hard water helps, but allow it to cool before using it to water your plants.

The best method, when using tap water, is to fill a few containers in advance, each time you water, and leave them for the next watering session for a minimum of 24 hours to allow the temperature to equalize and the chlorine to evaporate.

Potting mixes

Compost, potting soil and potting medium are all terms used to describe the material in which plants grow, and they're all accurate. I prefer to use the term potting mix because that is what it is, a mix, usually of more than one component, used for potted plants for indoor gardens.

The following is a brief breakdown of the most common potting mixes available at your local garden center or department store. A packaged potting mix is most convenient, but you can also mix your own combinations together if necessary. The ingredients are all quite common and easy to find. However, if you choose to create your own mix, don't use soil from your garden. It isn't sterile and will become too compacted for your houseplants.

Different plants have specific potting mix preferences. Some prefer a soil-based potting mix while others thrive in a soil-less mix made up primarily of peat moss. The choice of mix available at your local garden center can be overwhelming. The potting mix you choose serves as a physical support, a reservoir for nutrients and moisture and a support system for a variety of beneficial microorganisms. It may also perform other functions beneficial to your plant's specific needs and requirements, such as providing superior drainage, air circulation and support. Each mix will offer different elements beneficial for each plant.

Left to right: absorbent water polymers, soil-less potting mix, soil-based potting mix

There are four basic mixes. The two most common potting mixes are soil-based mixes and peat moss– or soil-less mixes. The two additional mixes are orchid mixes and cactus/succulent mixes. Different manufacturers will add different components to their mixes, and you may have to experiment to determine which is best for you and your plants.

Soil-based or loam-based mixes are often made up of sterilized soil with added sand, peat and fertilizers to add structure and nutrient value. Soil-based mixes have better water retention value but remain wet for longer periods. These weightier mixes provide added stability for larger specimen plants.

Peat-based mixes or soil-less mixes are often made up of peat moss or peat

moss substitutes with added fertilizers, sand, perlite, vermiculite and the like. There are even mixes with added slow-release fertilizer. I prefer not to recommend the fertilizer-amended products. They're often expensive, and even though the fertilizer is beneficial during the plant's active growth cycle, it is not necessarily a benefit when a plant's growth activity decreases or stops for a winter rest or dormancy. Although soil-less mixes have little in the way of nutrient value, they can be supplemented with a good fertilizing program.

Potting mix for epiphytic orchids is often a mix of bark chips, sphagnum moss and perlite, or a combination of osmunda fiber and peat moss, which allows the water to run over the roots without the mix retaining any moisture, thus providing great air circulation and support. The cactus/succulent potting mix is made up of a general mix with a high content of sand and grit for superior drainage.

Other materials added to potting mixes can include water-absorbing crystals or polymers, coir-based compost (shredded coconut shell), and so on. However, the basics are most important! The mix you choose should offer great drainage, structure, air movement capabilities and water retention value. Just about every other component can be improved with amendments, including sand for drainage.

Left: a *Phalaenopsis* orchid growing in orchid medium

Containers

Containers come in every shape, size and color imaginable. Nursery pots and decorative pots are both practical containers, but each serves a different purpose. The nursery pot is the green, brown or black, plain pot the plant comes in. It has adequate drainage, stability and space. The plant should usually remain in the nursery pot, and when you repot, simply move up to a larger nursery pot. The nursery pot can be placed into a decorative pot or container. The decorative container is the hardscape that completes, contrasts or complements the plant's natural form. You can use just about anything as a decorative container, including baskets, antique tins, bowls, interesting boxes and shallow dishes. Use your imagination! Some decorative containers are not suitable for direct planting, and most have little or no drainage capability. In some instances, however, you may plant the specimen directly into a decorative container.

When the nursery pot is exposed, you can disguise the pot with moss as a finishing touch. One thing to consider when choosing a decorative container is a place for the water to drain away from the rootball. You may have to line the interior of a decorative container if it's not waterproof, or place a saucer in the bottom to catch the run off. If the container is round or rectangular, there are many, generally inexpensive, and even ornamental, drainage trays available to slip under your decorative container to ensure the run off doesn't damage the surface it's sitting on.

Some devotees prefer clay pots to plastic. There are advantages to both, and choosing between them can sometimes depend on the plant. A clay pot adds weight, thereby providing more stability. Because of the porous nature of the material, you are less likely to overwater a plant in a clay pot; also salts will be leached away from the moist potting mix. However, the porous nature also means that plants are prone to drying out more quickly. Clay pots are also more difficult to clean and disinfect, they're more fragile and they retain moisture that can damage surfaces they're placed upon.

On the other hand, plastic pots are lightweight and less prone to breaking. Rootballs will generally retain moisture for longer periods and plastic pots are much easier to clean and disinfect. They're less expensive, available in more standardized sizes and come in a wide variety of colors and styles. Which type you choose depends a little on your plant and a little on your taste and budget.

Repotting

You'll often see references made to potting on, potting up and repotting—all have slightly different meanings. When a seedling or plant is planted into its first pot, this is **potting up**. **Potting on** takes place when a plant moves up into a slightly larger pot. **Repotting** occurs when a plant cannot be moved up into the next pot size, so the rootball is reduced in size, and is then returned to its former pot with new potting mix.

Repotting is also a general term. In some cases you won't know whether to pot on or repot until you can examine the rootball. With experience, you'll know when a plant would be better in a larger pot or left where it is.

Eventually there comes a time to repot every plant. Spring is often the best time to repot because it allows the plant an entire growing season to settle into its new environment, to produce enough roots and to prepare for its resting period or dormancy.

A container can effectively stunt the growth of a healthy plant because the roots have nowhere else to go; this is markedly different from plants grown outdoors. Regardless of size, the pot contains only a small volume of potting mix, so there are few available nutrients, and little space and water compared to planting in the ground. Potting mixes are sterile, eliminating any harmful organisms, pests and competition from weeds. Within a short period of time, nutrients will be used up by the plant and flushed out the bottom, so make sure to start a feeding routine during the growing season, soon after repotting a plant, to replenish what's lacking.

Repotting isn't always an annual job. Plants should be repotted only when necessary. Some plants actually

repotting a rootbound plant

prefer to be rootbound because it encourages flowering, but there are signs that indicate it's time to repot, including the slowing down of stem and foliar growth during the active growth cycle, the need to water more frequently, the almost daily drying out of the rootball and the growth of the roots through the drainage holes. To confirm that it's time to repot, gently remove the rootball from the pot to examine the root system. If the rootball consists of more roots than soil, or is a solid plug or mass of roots, it's time to move it up to a larger pot. If the rootball isn't rootbound, simply place it back into the pot. Often vigorously growing plants should be repotted or potted up annually in spring; slower growing plants, or plants with shallow or small root systems, need potting up less often.

Removing the rootball from the pot is an important technique to master. Make sure that the rootball is moist before removing it from the pot.

Place the palm of your hand over the surface of the rootball with the stems between your fingers. Gently invert the pot with your hand in place and pull the rootball from the pot, or push it through from the bottom.

You may have to gently tap the edge of the pot on a table or counter, or give the pot a gentle squeeze, to loosen the sides of the pot. If it resists coming out, slide a sharp knife along the inside edge of the pot and gently pull the rootball out. Larger plants should be laid on their sides and gently rolled from side to side to loosen the outer edge of the rootball from the pot. The rootball can then be gently pulled free.

If the pot that the rootball is about to go into has been used before, thoroughly scrub it out and disinfect it with a 10% bleach solution prior to use. Bleach only non-porous pots and containers; do not bleach clay unless it is glazed inside and out. Clay pots should also be soaked in water for at least 12 hours prior to potting; otherwise, the porous clay will absorb much of the water from the newly repotted rootball.

Cover the drainage hole with fine screen mesh or pieces of broken pot to prevent the newly added potting mix from washing out through the hole. Add new potting mix to the bottom of the pot and place the rootball into the pot on top of the new mix. Add or remove a little mix at the bottom to raise or lower the rootball so there is a gap between the top of the rootball and the rim of the pot. Once the rootball is at an appropriate height, gently tease some of the roots away from the clump, along the sides and bottom. Place the rootball back into the new pot and slowly fill the gap along the sides with mix until level with the top of the rootball. Do not push the mix down the sides with your fingers, or you could compact the newly added mix. Gently tap the bottom of the pot on a hard surface to knock the mix down, effectively removing any air pockets. Add just enough mix to

dust the top of the rootball so it remains level with the newly added mix. Now you can gently firm the mix with your fingers. Water thoroughly and you're done.

Another technique that is frequently used is the pot-in-pot method. It is similar to the first, but rather than

measuring depth with the rootball, you measure it by placing the empty former pot on top of the newly added mix and then filling in the side gaps with the pot still in the middle.

Then you slip the pot out and drop the rootball in its place.

Just before removing the pot, however, put a little pressure on the inside walls and bottom of the inner pot to lightly compress the newly added mix, preventing it from collapsing after the inner pot is removed. Now lightly dust the top with mix and water thoroughly.

When potting up a tiny seedling or newly rooted cutting, you need to determine what size pot to use. It is

best to use a seed or seedling potting mix rather than an all-purpose mix. A seed/seedling mix has a finer texture than a standard mix, with better drainage and moisture-retentive qualities. If the seedling or cutting is quite small, choose the smallest-sized nursery pot available that fits. A 2^1/$_2$" (6.4 cm) pot may be best to start with. If you have more than one seedling, you could group the seedlings/cuttings together and place them into a 4" (10 cm) pot, which is usually easier to find. Be sure not to plant it too deeply. The soil level should be to the top of the plug or where the roots begin. Water thoroughly, and remember that a smaller pot will dry out more quickly than a larger pot owing to the reduced volume of potting mix. Keep it consistently moist.

Inspect the root system from time to time by gently inverting the pot and tipping the rootball into the palm of your hand. Once the roots have made it to the edges or bottom of the pot, the plant can make the transition into a larger pot. The time it takes a plant to outgrow its pot will depend on a number of factors, including its natural growth rate, environmental conditions and time of year. Smaller plants will need to be potted on or repotted more frequently than larger plants.

Once plants have reached their mature indoor size, you may only have to topdress the rootball rather than repot it. Simply loosen the mix with a fork, remove the top few inches/centimeters of old mix and refresh with the same depth of new mix. This will enable most plants to remain in the same container for years.

The last method, repotting a plant back into its existing pot, works best for plants that prefer to be a little rootbound. Remove the rootbound rootball from the pot. Gently remove some

of the existing mix from the rootball with your fingers. Then slice a strip of rootball away with a sharp knife. Now the smaller rootball can be returned to

the same pot with newly refreshed potting mix using the previously mentioned process.

Training and supports

Plants can be trained using a variety of methods and techniques. Training encourages a plant to conform to a certain size or shape or to grow in a particular direction. Pruning and using supports are ways to train plants, most of which will require some form of training throughout their lives.

Trailing, creeping, scrambling and procumbent plants can be trained to grow vertically or can be left to cascade over the edges of their containers. Vertical growth can be supported by a stake, moss pole, topiary form, hoop or trellis. Any trailing or vine-like plant can be trained on any of these forms or supports; it just depends on your preferences. You could attach the twining stems of an English ivy to a hoop form and train it to conform to that shape. Philodendrons are often trained onto moss poles because the stems are less pliable, have aerial roots and are sometimes too thick to attach to a smaller form. The moss pole also adds stability to the vigorous stems and foliage. Paper flower is less apt to grow vertically on anything but a trellis or group of stakes because of its tough stems. Plants with smaller foliage and wiry stems are best trained onto topiary and hoop forms.

Stakes are frequently used to support tall, top-heavy flowers or single stems with little weight. Stakes are also useful when placed into a pot in the form of a teepee, tied with twine at the top. The stems may attach themselves with tendrils, but may need direction from time to time. Plants with no means of grasping onto the support will need additional support and direction from a soft tie or garden twine. A soft, flexible tie will prevent the stem from becoming damaged while forcing it to go in the desired direction. Bamboo and plastic covered steel stakes are

an inexpensive way to support vines in a less formal way, while still providing a vertical element for small and large plants.

Moss poles are ideal for plants with heavier stems, larger foliage and aerial roots. Aerial roots attach themselves directly into the moss, adding extra support. The stems can be attached with tiny metal pins to ensure that they remain attached to the pole. Trellises and stakes are good supports for plants with less flexible stems; hoops and topiary forms are best for lightweight, flexible stems with smaller leaves. If your plant has no tendrils, you will have to continue attaching the stems to the pole; otherwise, the plant will begin to lose its shape.

Another type of training often used for bushy, shrubby plants involves a little pruning and pinching to maintain the plant's shape and size.

Houseplants do not often require pruning, but to maintain a topiary or standard form, for example, you need to shape the head of the plant with pruning. Pinching the growing tips out from time to time will stimulate new buds into growth. The result is a bushier, shapelier plant that will often bear more flowers than plants that have been left to their own devices. Pinching back trailing stems will also encourage fuller growth in the center. Trailing stems shouldn't be allowed to get too long, though the lengths can vary from genus to genus. A basic rule is not to allow the trailing stems to grow much longer than the height of the container. This allows the plant to remain full rather than becoming spindly and straggly. Deadheading falls into both training and grooming categories. Removing spent flowerheads also encourages further blooming and a bushier growth habit, and it prevents the plant from going to seed. If the flowers are permitted to set seed, the plant's energy reserves are tapped, which signals to the plant that its blooming cycle is over and prevents future flushes of flowers. Remove the stems just above the area where a leaf joins the stem. Allow flowers that produce ornamental fruits, including ornamental peppers, to remain, so the fruits can form and show off their attributes.

Pruning

Training, pruning and grooming are all related. Pruning is sometimes necessary to train a woody ornamental into a particular form. Pinching back and deadheading are pruning techniques. Pruning is also used to remove dead, diseased or unsightly portions of the plant. It is an acquired skill that is very easy and, with practice, will become second nature. Pruning tools can include scissors, pruners, and the best pruning tool for indoor gardening, your thumbnail and the tip of your index finger.

Plants with long, trailing stems can begin to look straggly over time. When the trailers become too long and the leaves along the stems are emerging further and further apart, it's time to pinch them back. Shorten them by pinching back the straggly stems by at least half. If there are a great number of stems to be pruned

back, pinch only one-third of the stems first. In the following month, pinch back the next third and then the last third in the month after that. This puts less stress on the plant and allows it to gradually accept the change without pushing out a flush of new, lanky growth. You can also trim a few of the stems back to the potting mix to encourage new growth from the base. To encourage a bushier growth habit and to prevent a trailing plant from becoming straggly, pinch out the growing tips periodically. Allowing the trailers to grow to unreasonable lengths is stressful for the plant. The growth habit is affected and the result is an unsightly plant.

There is a proper and improper way to prune. Pruning bushy plants from time to time will maintain their full shape, preventing them from becoming too large and spindly. Pinching out the growing tips at least once a year stimulates the growth of new buds in the leaf axils below. The result is a bushier, more compact plant that will often bear more flowers and have a more pleasing shape.

Pinching out the growing tips can usually be done with your thumbnail, but if the stem is too thick, use pruners or scissors to make a clean cut. The cut should be made just above the first or second outward node, where the leaves join the stem.

Some plants prefer to be pruned or pinched back regularly, regardless of the time of year, while others will tolerate it only once or twice a year at the beginning of the growth cycle in spring. It may be necessary to cut back woody plants such as figs and gardenias with pruners or scissors from time to time. Do not remove flower buds carried at the ends of the stems or you will have a flowering plant without flowers.

Cleanliness is imperative when pruning anything, and preparation is a must. When pruning, always have a paper towel at hand to remove any oozing sap from the freshly cut stems. Ficus plants will 'bleed' when cut, and the sap can stain fabrics and carpet. Ensure that your pruners, scissors and fingernails are clean before making any cuts to prevent the spread of disease and bacteria. A drop sheet may also be handy for easier cleanup when removing growth from any plant. Pruning houseplants isn't a big job and requires little time. It will add life to your plants and will help to maintain their shape.

Cleaning and grooming

Regularly cleaning and grooming your plants is well worth the effort because your plants will not only look better, they'll be better able to fight disease, insect infestations and adverse conditions. It also gives you the opportunity to closely inspect the entire plant for insect infestations and disease. It will take little of your time if you develop a routine, but if you let it get away from you, it could become a huge task,

depending on how many plants you have. I do a little grooming each day, removing a dead leaf or flower here and there, or quickly dusting broad leaves.

Cleaning and grooming techniques are simple and easy to perform. Techniques vary, but I recommend the following. You will need very little in the way of supplies. Create a little grooming kit, made up of a soft sponge, paper towels, a soft cloth, a feather duster, sharp scissors, garden twine, bamboo stakes, a small garbage bag, a mister, small indoor gardening tools and a soft paint brush.

Commercial leaf shine and cleaning products are available to clean dust off leaves, but I prefer to use a damp sponge, dry cloth or paper towel for this purpose. Dust acts like a filter, turning bright light into bright filtered light, reducing its potency. Simply removing dust from the surface of the leaves allows more light, and therefore more fuel, to reach the plant. It also keeps the stomata or pores from clogging up, which enables the transfer of oxygen and carbon dioxide to flow more freely. Cleaning and grooming extends to your windows—a clean window allows more light to pass through than a dirty, grimy one.

To remove dust and dirt from foliage, with the palm of your hand support the underside of the leaf, and then wipe or gently rub it with a sponge or cloth. A dry cloth or paper towel is quite effective when removing dust and dirt that hasn't adhered to the leaves, but some leaf surfaces are apt

to hold onto the dust. A damp sponge works well in this situation, sometimes followed by a dry, soft cloth for polishing. These tools should remove any dust or dirt from smooth foliage.

A feather duster is handy when used with discretion. Be careful not to dust a plant with spider mites because the mites will transfer from the duster to each and every plant afterwards. I recommend the feather duster only to experienced indoor gardeners, but it can be the ideal tool to keep an already thoroughly cleaned plant tidy.

A small paintbrush is ideal for cleaning hairy foliage. The bristles allow you to get in between the hairs to remove dust and dirt. Do not wet hairy foliage because it may become spotted and damaged.

Some leaves and flowers will eventually have to be removed from every plant. Leaves should be removed at the point from where they emerge; do not leave a partial stem behind to spoil the

appearance. This is also true for dead-heading. When removing a flower, remove the stem as well. Remove individual flowers as they fade from within a cluster. Once the entire cluster has finished its cycle, remove it, stem and

all. Deadheading will discourage the onset of diseases and problems caused by fungus that forms on spent flowers and later spreads to the foliage.

Plants can benefit from a gentle shower or bath from time to time to remove all dust, debris and evidence of insect infestation. Smaller plants can be washed under the tap or swished about

in a sink or container of water. Larger plants are easier to get into the shower. Ensure that the water temperature is

Left, clockwise from top, organic fertilizers: Gaia Green glacial rock dust, earthworm castings, all purpose fertilizer. Right, clockwise from top, synthetic fertilizers: liquid concentrate 5-15-15 root booster, all purpose water soluable fertilizer, fertilizer spikes.

tepid, not warm or cold, and running at a lower pressure. Handheld showerheads are ideal because you can adjust the water pressure, and you have the flexibility to spray underneath the leaves. Allow the plants to drip dry in a cool area with little exposure to light to prevent the wet foliage from scorching in bright light. Once the leaves are dry, you can return the plants to their original space. Be careful when taking plants outdoors for a bath. Changes in temperature, light and water pressure may be too much and could result in an irreversibly damaged plant.

Fertilizers and amendments

Fertilizing is a bit of a contentious issue for those in the horticultural world—some people advocate regular synthetic fertilizer and others advocate the use of organic amendments. I fall somewhere in the middle. Also, my fertilizing practices outdoors are somewhat different than that of my indoor gardening routine. The following is what I recommend for the beginner indoor gardener.

Why we fertilize

Providing nutrients for your plants is important, especially when they are grown in containers. The small volume of potting mix holds few nutrients, and these nutrients are simultaneously being used and flushed out of the bottom of the pot with every watering, year-round. Granted there are tiny amounts of minor and trace elements available in our water, the air and often in the potting mix, but supplemental applications of nutrients are a benefit in the long run. Nutrients should be replaced consistently throughout the growing season, from spring to fall while the plant is actively growing.

Fertilizers are composed of three major elements: nitrogen, phosphorus and potassium. These aid a plant in absorbing light to produce healthier leaves, stems, flowers and fruit, and contribute to a plant's energy reserves for future use. Fertilizer also helps a plant build up resistance to insects, pests and disease. Plants do not require fertilizer to live, but using fertilizer and organic amendments helps plants to flourish. A plant with depleted nutrient levels may be smaller, grow more slowly and produce fewer flowers, but it will still grow. Plants grown with excessive amounts of fertilizer will appear much the same or with lush, vulnerable flushes of growth, along with signs of damage, including brown tips, weak growth and root damage.

Moderation and knowing what to use when are the keys to success.

Availability and composition

Many different fertilizers are available, each with its own composition, application and frequency. It can be a little overwhelming to the beginner. There are synthetic and organic fertilizers, as well as powders, crystals, liquids, spikes and tablets. Concentrated liquids, crystals and powders are a little more cost efficient and have a more immediate effect, while slow-release products should be combined with potting mix when planting. Slow release granules, pellets and spikes are often effective for three to six months or more. But the plant may not use the fertilizer for that long, so it may build up in the soil. It's also difficult to know when to replace slow-release fertilizers. Fertilizer spikes and tabs also tend to release concentrated amounts in one spot, killing the neighboring roots.

Calling fertilizers 'plant food' is a misnomer. Completely synthetic fertilizers are not food but rather are equivalent to mineral supplements for plants. These include standard water-soluble and slow-release products available at your local garden center. Other products are simple to use, beneficial to the plant and can provide better results. Organic amendments include mycorrhizal fungi, organic fertilizer blends, compost tea, earthworm castings and more. These products are slowly becoming more available.

Fertilizers have three major elements, which are represented by three numbers listed on the packaging. The first number is nitrogen, the second is phosphorus and the third is potassium. You'll become familiar with certain combinations, including 20-20-20, which is a balanced fertilizer composed of 20 parts of each element. A flowering fertilizer often has a higher middle number. A 15-30-15 is 15 parts nitrogen, 30 parts phosphorus and 15 parts potassium. Organic fertilizers have much lower numbers but are just as effective.

The three major elements all assist in plant growth. Nitrogen (N) is critical in the production of chlorophyll, which allows plants to better absorb light, their primary source of energy. Nitrogen also aids in the production of new, healthy stems and foliage. However, excessive nitrogen will promote weak flushes of growth that are more vulnerable to pests and disease. It can also burn the roots and foliage.

Phosphorus (P) is beneficial to flower and fruit development, improving their size, longevity and coloration.

Potassium (K) aids in energy storage and helps build a stronger resistance to pests and disease.

Most complete fertilizers also include small amounts of minor elements, including calcium, magnesium and sulfur. Trace elements, also known as micronutrients, are also present in even smaller quantities. Some of the more common micronutrients are iron, manganese and copper. Often the

staghorn ferns and zebra plant (*Aphelandra*).

Synthetic fertilizers are mostly composed of salts, which will eventually need to be flushed out of the rootball because of the salt buildup from regular or excessive applications. Salts can also kill most soil microorganisms, and even though there may be fewer microorganisms in pot culture, their role is essential to the distribution of nutrients and water to a plant's roots. A plant will become more reliant on synthetic fertilizers as the microorganisms decrease in numbers.

Because sterilized potting mixes contain few microorganisms, there are products on the market that add microorganisms back into soil. These microorganisms are known as mycorrhizal fungi along with other beneficial organisms. Mycorrhizal fungi colonize a plant's root system by creating a network that increases its capacity to absorb water and nutrients such as phosphorus, copper and zinc. This process, in turn, enhances growth and favors rapid development of roots and plants. It's best not to use synthetic fertilizers, especially those high in phosphorus, in conjunction with mycorrhizal-enhanced products because the microorganisms are likely to be killed off, rendering the fungi useless. Compost and unsterilized organic amendments have a high percentage of mycorrhizae as well.

micronutrients are negligible only because they're usually available in city water and standard potting mixes.

Specialized fertilizers are available for just about every type of plant, but the two that stand out are tomato fertilizer and acid-based fertilizer. Often the use of a complete fertilizer will prevent mineral deficiencies if used once or twice during the growing season, but for indoor gardening it's best to alternate between these specialized fertilizers and a complete fertilizer during the short time available. Tomato fertilizer is higher in potassium, which is ideal towards the end of the growing season as your plants begins to prepare for the winter ahead. This fertilizer is also perfect for cacti and succulents all season long. Acid-based fertilizers are better suited to a limited number of plants that prefer acidic growing conditions, including azaleas, calamondin, camellias, gardenia, hydrangeas,

How to fertilize

Application rates and frequency of application recommended on synthetic fertilizer packaging are for plants in ideal conditions. Cut the recommended dose by half or more, but use the same amount of water. Under less than ideal growing conditions, plants are less likely to absorb large amounts of fertilizer, which will result in a buildup of unused fertilizer in the soil, and can cause irreversible damage. Flowering and fruiting plants benefit from higher quantities of fertilizer as well as additional light, water and humidity.

Organic fertilizers contain the same elements but in an organic form and in smaller quantities or percentages, but these shouldn't be used excessively either. Follow the recommended rates on the packaging. If there is no packaging, as with compost tea, for example, you may need to research the correct dosage. Remember, less is more—you can add more, but you can't take excess away.

When to fertilize

Newly purchased plants will almost certainly have residual fertilizer in their soil, so it's not necessary to fertilize them for several months, and then only during the growing season. It will take months for a new plant to acclimatize to its new environment, so it will be a little vulnerable during this time. Plants are often damaged or killed owing to excessive fertilizing rather than a lack of fertilizer.

If using a synthetic fertilizer, try to alternate formulations throughout the growing season. Start the season with an all-purpose mix for the first month, switch to a flowering plant fertilizer for the subsequent months and end the season with a tomato fertilizer in late summer or early fall. Plants do not need fertilizer during winter unless it's very diluted because they are resting and not growing much. Plants grown under grow lights can be fertilized year-round, however, because they don't really experience a rest period.

Weakened plants should not be fertilized until they regain some stability. This includes plants recovering from any form of shock, plants recently affected by pests or disease and newly transplanted or repotted plants. To prevent burning, never apply any type of fertilizer to dry soil.

A small group of plants can only be fertilized through their leaves with a foliar feeding. Plants are only capable of absorbing a minute quantity of fertilizer through their foliage and you have to be careful what plants you use this method on. Specialized fertilizer products made for this purpose and more standardized products, with foliar feed application recommendations on the packaging, are available. Epiphytic orchids and bromeliads are part of the small group that will benefit from this method.

Fertilizing your plants will soon become routine. Just remember that it's not the end of the world if you forget an application or neglect to fertilize all season long—a little goes a long way and your plants will survive without it.

Indoors to Outdoors and Outdoors to Indoors: Making a Smooth Transition

Most plants will benefit from a visit outdoors in summer—flowering plants will flourish; thin, faded plants will fill out with lush, new growth; and at the end of the season, your plants will be ready for another winter indoors.

However, you must be careful during the move and allow them time to acclimatize. Generally, difficulties arise when a plant is moved to a patio or balcony without a gradual and safe transition to its temporary outside home or when a plant is placed in a location where conditions are too harsh. With a little patience and the right information, you'll be able to successfully move a plant or two outdoors for a summer boost.

To prevent damage, plants need to be moved outside gradually rather than in one fell swoop. First, move them into a protected, semi-shady location and allow them to acclimatize there for a day or two. Then move them into a slightly brighter location with a little less protection and allow them to acclimatize again. Continue

this process until your plants are in their new summer location, even if it takes a week or two.

Choose a location outside that resembles the inside space. If your croton needs an extra boost of sunlight to enhance coloration that's faded over the winter months, choose a spot in bright light with a short period of direct sunlight. To prevent damage, choose a location with slightly less light than recommended.

The best candidates for a summer vacation outdoors are plants with fleshy or thick leaves, flowering plants, cacti and succulents and plants that have become a little thin over winter. Plants with thin leaves are more susceptible to burning.

Plants moved outside may have to be watered more often. Monitor their progress, and be prepared to slowly move them back into a shadier, protected location, or even back inside, if temperatures become too hot or if plants begin to show signs of damage.

At the end of the season, your plants will have to make the trek back indoors. Be careful not to leave them out for too long at the end of summer or early fall. Most houseplants won't tolerate even a light frost, so pay attention to forecasts and frost dates and bring them in sooner rather than later. Re-acclimatizing your plants to their original indoor environment takes only half the time. Inspect every inch of the plant for pests prior to bringing it back in. If possible, rinse the entire plant to prevent a potential insect infestation. If you do find evidence of a pest or disease, determine the specific problem, then treat as necessary and quarantine the plant for a short time before returning it to its original location.

When you go away

The following techniques will keep your plants thriving for up to two weeks without you having to hire a plant-sitter. Experiment with them while you're at home to see what works best for you.

Plants with reservoir-like root systems or succulent foliage should be watered thoroughly and deeply just prior to leaving. Other plants are less prepared to recover from an excessively dry rootball for any period of time. If you're absent often, there are ways to keep your plants watered that require only a small investment and will give you peace of mind while you're away.

Capillary matting is a cost-efficient way of keeping the rootballs of your plants moist for weeks. Fill your

capillary matting, deep water probe, aqua probe

kitchen sink with water and place half the matting on the sink bottom and half on a drainboard beside the sink. Place your plants on the drainboard. Water is drawn from the sink up to the drainboard matting by capillary action. This method works well for plants in plastic pots with more than one drainage hole—the holes will draw the water into the rootball until the sink runs dry. This method is not useful for plants in clay pots because most of the moisture is absorbed by the clay rather than by the rootball.

Small groups of plants that can't be put beside your sink can also benefit from this method. Cut your matting into strips. Place one end of the strip into a container of water and the other well into the rootball. Be sure the rootball is already moist prior to pushing the matting end into the compost. Depending on the size of the water reservoir, you can wick water to several plants from one container.

Self-watering pots resemble other pots on the outside but are constructed to allow a plant to water itself during your absence. The bottom of the pot acts as the wicking system. The wick, which is inserted through the bottom of the rootball when initially planted, draws water up into the rootball. This only takes place when there is sufficient water in the reservoir. This style of pot is handy for short periods of time but is not always best for long-term use, especially for the beginning gardener, because the pot may be feeding water to the rootball when it's not needed.

Ceramic mushrooms use capillary action as well and are quite effective. They draw water from a separate source through a wick into the ceramic portion that is pushed into the rootball.

Porous irrigators are small, bulbous, open-ended devices made of a material like clay or ceramic. Buried into the rootball up to the opening and then filled with water, they leach the moisture into the rootball through the porous material. These are effective for short absences, such as a weekend.

A simple wicking system is also effective. This method works very well for pots no larger than 6" (15 cm) in diameter. Cut a length of wick double the depth of the pot. Thread the wick through a large needle, such as an upholstery needle, and draw it up through the drainage hole and diagonally through the rootball to the top, so one end is slightly above the surface. The number of wicks will depend on the size of the pot. Two

may be sufficient for a 6" (15 cm) diameter pot. The long ends should be dangling from the drainage hole in the bottom. Place the pot on a platform in your kitchen sink, with the wicks in the water and touching the bottom of the sink. The water level in the sink should not be higher than the bottom of the pot, but the higher the water level, the longer the water will wick up into the rootball.

Well-watered, smaller plants can be placed into a sealed, inflated bag to maintain a moist environment. Be sure the leaves aren't touching the sides of the bag, and remove all spent leaves, stems and flowers. Don't entrap the plant for too long because rot and mold can set in. Move it into a location with moderate light but without direct sunlight to ensure the plant is not damaged from the sealed environment heating up. This method isn't appropriate for plants such as cacti or succulents.

If you have a brightly lit bathroom, the bricks-in-the-bathtub technique works well for a weekend. Place a layer or two of bricks wide enough to support as many plants as necessary in the bottom of your bathtub. Then fill the tub with water until it reaches the upper edge of the bricks without going over the top. Place your thoroughly watered plants on top of the bricks, and the water will wick through the porous bricks into the bottom of the pot through the drainage holes. This method works best for plastic pots; it is not recommended for clay pots.

Propagation

Almost every houseplant can be reproduced by a variety of means, either from an existing plant or from scratch. Seeding is a propagation technique, but there are more reliable, quicker and easier methods of propagating indoor plants. The seed is often impossible to find, it may take months to germinate and the process may require a big commitment of time and space on your part. We will focus here, instead, on vegetative forms of propagation such as cuttings, division, offsets and plantlets and layering.

Propagating by cuttings takes little time, space or skill. Different types of cuttings include stem cuttings, leaf cuttings and cane cuttings. Techniques are plant-specific because each plant is unique. The supplies needed to take cuttings include prepared seed starter or cuttings potting mix; a mister bottle; a watering can; sharp scissors; pruners or a sharp blade; rooting hormone; a freshly disinfected small pot or flat, small bamboo stakes; small clear plastic bags; elastics; blank tags; a permanent black marker and a spare pencil.

Propagating by stem or tip cuttings is common for plants that produce branches. Use this technique in spring as follows:

- Fill your container with the prepared seed starter or cuttings potting mix. Use the mister bottle to moisten just the top two thirds of the mix. Gently firm the mix with your fingertips to remove air pockets.
- Depending on the size of the parent plant, the cutting should be 4–6" (10–15 cm) long, with at least two to three nodes (the node is where the leaf joins the stem).
- Cut the stem just above the bottom node and remove the foliage from the two lower nodes, leaving only a bit of foliage on the tip.
- Dip the cut end and the lowest node of the cutting into the rooting hormone. Gently tap the cutting to remove excess rooting hormone.

- Poke the end of the pencil into the mix to create a hole. Insert the cutting into the hole and gently firm the mix around the stem to remove air pockets and to ensure potting mix to stem contact.
- Depending on the size of the pot, repeat this process two to four times in one pot.
- Moisten the mix more thoroughly with your mister bottle.
- Place two or three stakes, slightly taller than the cuttings, into the mix around the perimeter of the pot.
- Place the plastic bag over top of the stakes, trying not to make contact with the cuttings.

- Secure the bag with the elastic to create a greenhouse. Place in a location with moderate light and no direct sunlight.
- Open the bag from time to time if condensation begins to build; don't allow the potting mix to dry out.
- Remove the bag and stakes after the roots have formed.

Cuttings from certain plants will form a new root system very quickly while others may take months. It is important to maintain a consistent environment for newly rooting cuttings. After several weeks or months, you can peek occasionally to see whether roots have begun to form by gently removing the pot from the rootball. If the firm, creamy white roots have reached the edge of the pot, you'll know that it's time to remove the bag and stakes. Your new plant now has its own root system and can be treated as a normal plant.

Leaf cuttings are appropriate for those plants without branches and for stemless plants, where the leaf base sits directly on the crown of the plant. There are three different types of leaf cuttings that are specific to different plants.

Leaf cuttings that include the stem or stalk are best for begonias other than *B. rex*, *Peperomia* species without a branching habit and African violets.

Leaf cuttings using the whole leaf are often used for succulent plants, including jade plants.

Leaf cuttings using only part of the leaf are used for plants with stemless leaves, including snake plant and cape primrose. Rex begonias and gloxinia are two exceptions to this rule.

Leaf cuttings with the stem attached are propagated using the following process:

- Fill a newly disinfected small pot with seed starter or cuttings potting mix, moisten the mix with the mister bottle and gently firm the mix down with your fingertips to remove air pockets.
- Make a hole in the mix with the end of the pencil.
- Cut the stem of a mature leaf about 2" (5.1 cm) from the base of the leaf.

- Dip the freshly cut stem into the rooting hormone and place into the hole up to the base of the leaf; repeat two to four times depending on pot size.
- Gently firm the mix around the stem; water just enough to remoisten the mix.

- Place the short stakes into the mix around the perimeter of the pot so they stand above the leaves.
- Place the bag over the stakes and fasten the bottom with the elastic.
- Keep the cuttings warm and moist and place the pot in a location with moderate light but no direct sunlight for a month or two.
- Peek after a month or so to see if the roots have reached the edge of the pot. If so, remove the plastic bag and the stakes, and move the pot to the best location for that plant.

Whole leaf cuttings follow a very similar process.
- Remove a leaf from the stem, dip the exposed end into the rooting hormone and place into the moistened potting mix. Small succulent leaves can be laid on the surface and gently pressed down slightly into the moistened mix.
- Keep the leaf cuttings moist and warm and check for newly developed roots from time to time.

Leaf cuttings using only part of the leaf are easy to do, following this process:
- Fill a tray or a flat with the seed starter or cuttings potting mix, moisten thoroughly and gently firm with your fingertips.
- Remove a leaf from the plant and lay it face down on a cutting surface.
- Rounded or heart-shaped leaves can be cut into even squares or triangles and inserted into the mix with the edge that was nearest the leaf stalk facing downwards.
- Strap-shaped or narrow leaves should be cut into sections no wider than 2" (5.1 cm).
- The end of the section nearest the stalk can then be inserted into the mix.

- Cover the flat or tray with a clear plastic dome, keep moist and warm until the roots begin to form (usually a period of months).
- New plants will begin to form around the cutting, a clear indication that roots have been produced.
- The newly formed plants can then be potted into their own pots and treated like a normal plant.

Cane cuttings are easy to take and are useful when propagating some dracaenas and dumb canes. The process is as follows:

- Fill a small, disinfected pot with seed starter or cuttings potting mix.
- Moisten the top third and gently firm it down with your fingertips.
- Cut the thick stem into pieces approximately 2–3" (5.1–7.6 cm) long with at least one node; either insert the cutting vertically into the mix, or better, lay it horizontally, pressing the lower half into the mix.
- The leaf buds should be facing upwards and kept moist and warm.
- New foliage should begin to emerge from the cutting when it has developed a new root system.

Division is a quick and easy method of dividing a plant into two or more plants depending on the number of crowns and root available. This method is best for plants made up of a number of clumps or rosettes. All you need is a very sharp knife, potting mix suitable for the plant you're dividing and new pots for the new divisions.

- Remove the rootball from the pot.
- Remove some of the mix surrounding the roots. Closely inspect the rootball to determine if you can safely separate it into healthy portions. Each portion should have at

least one crown or growing point attached to plenty of roots.

- Gently pull apart some of the roots and begin to pull the rootball apart with your hands.
- Once you've determined where to make the break, gently tease the sections apart. Cut or snap any adjoining pieces if necessary to free one part from another.
- Be very careful not to damage the crowns or roots. If necessary, rinse some of the mix away for better access.
- Once apart, trim the larger roots if necessary but leave the smaller fibrous roots intact.

- Pot the separate portions individually in an appropriate mix and place in a location in moderate light with no direct sunlight until they've become newly established.
- Once they're rooted in and have begun to grow, they can be moved to a more appropriate location.

Offsets and plantlets

Offsets and plantlets are tiny new plants that are attached to the parent plant in a variety of ways. Plants that produce offsets and plantlets provide an easy method of propagation without having to sacrifice the parent plant. Bromeliads, for example, often produce offsets that are easily removed from the parent plant. Spider plants produce plantlets from dangling stems.

Offsets or pups, which resemble a tiny version of the parent plant, emerge from the main stem or crown of the plant or from a secondary stem that is produced close to the parent

plant. An offset is usually ready to be separated when it reaches one-quarter to one-third the size of the parent plant. This should take place during the active growth stage or in spring and summer. First, closely inspect where the two

plants are joined to determine where to cut. Remove the offset from the stem as close to the stem as possible using a sharp knife, being careful to preserve any roots that may be attached.

If there is a reasonable amount of root attached, the offset should only require potting up and a week or so to establish. If there is little or no root, however, the offset should be treated like a cutting.

Plantlets are also tiny versions of the parent plant, but they're attached by a variety of means including leaves, stems, flower stalks and stolons. Plantlets will produce roots where

they're allowed to make contact to the soil or potting mix. Peg down the base of the plantlet to some moistened seed starting or cuttings potting mix, using u-shaped pieces of wire to keep the stem in contact with the mix, and the plantlet will begin to produce roots. After the roots have formed and top growth has taken place, the plantlet can be cut from the runner or stem to which it is attached. Now the tiny plantlet can be treated as a new plant.

Plantlets that form on the leaves of their parent can be gently removed and planted up separately.

Layering

There are two simple layering techniques that are used for different purposes. Ordinary layering is used to propagate trailing plants often grown in hanging baskets. Air layering is used to propagate woody or thickly stemmed plants, especially when they grow too large and need a little bulk at the base.

Ordinary layering is ideal for plants that will root from the stem, which includes most climbing and creeping plants. This technique requires a few supplies: small, new pots; seed starting or cuttings potting mix; wire pins and sharp scissors or pruners. First, place the hanging plant on a table or stable surface and fill the new pots with potting mix. Moisten the mix and firm it down a little with your fingertips. Position the newly filled pots close to the parent plant. Select long, healthy stems covered in young growth, and using the wire pins, peg the stem at a node into the mix. A small, shallow cut made under the stem will speed up the rooting process by making good soil-to-stem contact. Firm the stem in place and moisten once again. After a month or so, there should be enough root in place to sever the new plant from the parent. Keep the new plant in moderate light, out of direct sunlight, until it is well established.

Air layering is ideal for tall, leggy plants with woody or thick stems. Thickly stemmed, mature dumb canes and *Ficus* species are common candidates. Air layering is a simple process but requires a bit of patience because it may take some time for the cut to root. The supplies necessary to begin air layering your plants are a sharp grafting or pocket knife; a handful of fresh, moist sphagnum moss; elastics or twist ties; a tiny paintbrush or cotton swab; rooting hormone for semi-ripe or woody cuttings; a one-foot square sheet of clear plastic and a mister bottle.

• First, make an upward cut about 1" (2.5 cm) long, cutting just under the layer of bark, just beneath a node.

- Wrap the plastic twice around the cut to create a pouch and fasten on the bottom end with the elastic or twist tie. It should not be too tight because it only has to hold the plastic in place.
- Dip the cotton swab or paintbrush into the rooting hormone and apply the product into the cut.

- Slip a small amount of moist moss into the slit. Use the rest around the stem where the cut was made.

- Moisten the moss again.
- Close the pouch at the top and fasten with another elastic or twist tie.
- Check the pouch weekly to ensure that the moss hasn't dried out. Once new roots are visible, cut the stem just below the rooted stem and pot either separately or into the existing pot to fill a bare gap, adding some density to the bottom of an otherwise old and bare plant. New shoots will likely form from the cut where the top was removed.

Propagating is fun, easy and economical. You'll have more plants than you know what to do with in no time.

Old and New Trends

As in other things, gardening trends come and go. The current resurgence of interest in indoor gardening has inspired several new trends. Bringing the outdoors in, for example, with ornamental grasses, tabletop bog gardens and aquatic plants in vases, is especially popular. The following gardening trends are easy to create,

require little care and will become focal points in your home.

Bottle gardens have taken on new forms. In the 1970s, my parents transformed a large bottle that once held crabapple wine into a bottle garden. This style is still common, but beautiful flowering plants in tall, cylindrical vases as living art pieces, miniature moss and lichen gardens in small decorative bottles, and even perennials and tropicals planted directly into glass art are the bottle gardens of the new millennium.

The terrarium has been used in indoor gardening for more than a century. It beautifully showcases prized plants and its enclosed, humid space is an ideal environment for moisture-loving plants. You can still find Victorian terrariums for more traditional settings, but terrariums with more contemporary designs are available today.

A simple, stout, cylindrical vase with a small, planted specimen surrounded by moss can act as a terrarium with an open top. The humidity is still contained around the plant and its unique display draws the eye.

Bringing the outdoors in can also be done by forcing branches and bulbs. This quick blast of color late in winter is your ticket to an early spring indoors. It's easy to do and relieves a winter-weary mind.

Just about any type of bulb can be forced into bloom by simulating outdoor conditions in a condensed time frame. Place planted bulbs into a cool place, like a cool garage or unheated basement, for a period of weeks to replicate winter dormancy. Pre-chilled tulip, hyacinth and daffodil bulbs are available from your local garden center in late winter, and sometimes earlier. Bulbs ideal for indoor forcing that require no chilling include *Narcissus tazetta*, *N. tazetta orientalis* and amaryllis, which is forced into bloom shortly before Christmas. As the days grow longer and the temperatures increase, greenery and spring flowers emerge that make a beautiful addition to the winter or spring holiday table.

Spring-flowering tree and shrub branches can be forced to bloom indoors to provide an architectural element with added color up to a month earlier than you

would get outdoors. When temperatures rise above freezing in late January and February, select and cut branches that have a reasonable number of plump buds from spring-flowering trees or shrubs. Place them in a decorative container and the warmth of the room will signal the buds to break open. A few of the more popular branches to force include *Forsythia*, *Prunus*, *Malus*, *Salix*, *Magnolia*, *Crataegus* and *Cercis*.

The vast majority of plants grown indoors have, historically, been grown for ornamental purposes only. This is beginning to change. The many people living in multi-dwelling buildings, condo complexes and shared dwellings that have little or no outdoor garden space can still enjoy fresh, edible plants by growing edible indoor gardens. Often edible garden plants are quick-growing varieties that can be easily replaced with something new as the seasons change.

Starting an edible indoor garden can be as simple as growing lettuce in a decorative container on your kitchen counter, with another seeded flat in the wings to replace it. Herbs have always been a favorite of indoor gardeners. Today, many new varieties and new growing techniques for year-round use are available. Wheat grass can be grown indoors for juicing. Herbal tea gardens are simple and offer a continuing selection of fresh herbs.

You can increase the availability of fruit-producing plants indoors by selecting citrus-bearing shrubs, including *Citrus meyeri* (Meyer lemon tree), and *Fortunella* (kumquat), among others.

Topiary forms of woody plants (*right*) are popular again as houseplants. Herbs like rosemary and myrtle are commonly found in garden centers in topiary or standard forms. They're often expensive, but the carefully trained balls of foliage take little time to maintain, plus they're beautiful as ornamentals or as culinary herbs. Most plants with smaller leaves and woody stems or branches can be trained into this form and will add elegance to any décor.

Bonsai is not a type of plant but a means of dwarfing trees in containers. Bonsai originated in China thousands of years ago, was later adopted by the Japanese as a decorative art, and remains popular today. The traditional Bonsai forms are still widely available and, with training, the avid student can become a Bonsai artist. For those who want the appearance of Bonsai without all the work, varieties are now available that require little pruning or training, often referred to as 'lazy man's Bonsai' (*left*). These specimens are chosen for their size, slow growth habit and overall form. They can be planted in a small container, and may require less water and space, but will eventually have to be repotted into a new container. Sago and parlor palms are two examples of plants that are readily available in this less traditional Bonsai form.

Tabletop gardens allow you to bring outdoor designs indoors on a smaller scale. With some imagination and a few supplies, you can choose a theme and simulate outdoor environments in your home, including bog gardens planted in shallow trays, succulent gardens, fairy gardens and water gardens. A bog garden, for example, is simple to construct using a decorative water-proof container. All you have to do is select plants conducive to your interior lighting conditions and add water.

The current popularity of fairies and folklore has led to the miniature garden becoming more popular. This is the ideal indoor garden for children. Adding fairytale characters to a miniature garden will challenge your children's imaginations and will introduce them to the wonderful world of gardening at an early age.

All it takes to create a miniature world for a winged fairy or a superhero is a glass bowl or globe, two or three miniature plants, fine decorative stone or pebbles and a few accessories, including a small figurine in scale with the plants. Get your kids involved with ideas, plant selection and planting and they'll have fun and learn about plants at the same time.

Plants grown for their idiosyncratic appearance or habit are fun for kids and adult enthusiasts alike, the collector or the beginner who wants something unique. Unusual plant varieties, which are becoming more prevalent and easier to find, include carnivorous plants like Venus fly trap, pitcher plant and sundew; plants sensitive to touch like the sensitive plant and *Biophytum*

sensitivum; and *Maranta* species that change position all day and night long. There are plants with fuzzy leaves and sticky flowers, plants displaying the oddest of colors and plants with foliage that emits a strange aroma when disturbed or in bloom.

There are many different ways to grow, train, display and experiment with plants in an indoor setting. Indoors you have all of the control and can create a unique environment for each and every plant. All it takes is a little knowledge and a lot of imagination. So have fun and start small. Before you know it, you'll be moving out furniture to make room for more wonderful plants.

sensitive plant before & after being touched

Insects, Pests and Diseases

Thankfully the number of pests and diseases affecting indoor plants is somewhat limited because the plants are being grown indoors. The few critters and potential problems you must contend with are relatively easy to get rid of, but you must first determine what the problem is before you're able to treat it.

The first line of defense in preventing the onset of disease and insect infestation is to properly care for your plants—give them what they need to stay healthy and strong, and they'll be of less interest to pests and diseases. Second, thoroughly check a plant for bugs and disease before buying it. If you bring a plant home with insects attached, you're setting yourself up for future problems. Quarantine a newly purchased plant from existing plants for a month or so, in a suitable spot. If anything turns up during this period, you can treat the problem without contaminating everything around it, or you can cut your losses by dumping the plant. Practice good cleaning and grooming habits because a clean plant is a healthier plant.

Following is a listing of the most common indoor pests and diseases and how to treat them effectively and safely. Certain less common problems, such as eelworms and rust, have not been included.

APHIDS

Aphids are green, brown, black, yellow, red or gray soft-bodied insects that are quite common and very easy to eradicate. Some are winged; others are not. Aphids are often found on the newest, most tender growth. They weaken the plant by sucking the sap from the stems and foliage. Signs of damage are foliar deformities and honeydew deposits left on lower leaves, which can lead to other problems. For example, sooty mold, a black fungus that grows on the sticky residue, limits the light quantities available to the plant and obstructs the pores or stomata on the surface of the leaves. Aphids reproduce at an alarming rate and are also known to transmit plant viruses.

Control: Rinse off the aphids and the honeydew with water; squish them with your fingers; spray with insecticidal soap, neem or pyrethrin-based insecticides.

BOTRYTIS

Gray mold (botrytis) is gray and fuzzy and easy to identify because it stands out on the foliage. It can affect all parts of a plant if conditions are humid and cool with poor air circulation. Plants with green, tender growth are especially susceptible.

Control: Prevention, by providing adequate air circulation and not overwatering, is the best method of control. Remove all infected parts, and if it's too far gone, dispose of the entire plant. Cut back on your watering, improve ventilation and avoid wetting the foliage of vulnerable plants.

CYCLAMEN MITES

Cyclamen mites are tiny creatures that are usually discovered long after their arrival. They aren't very common but are probably the most difficult to control. In masses, they appear as a thin layer of dust on the undersides of the leaves. These minute mites attack African violets and begonias. The damage results in stunted or deformed new growth and discolored flowers. Unlike red spider mites, cyclamen mites don't mind humidity or water and will continue to thrive.

Control: There is no product available on the market to kill this insect. Remove and destroy infested leaves if caught early enough. Discard completely infested plants.

DRAFTS

Drafts, both cold and hot, are problematic for many plants. Drafts can come from a number of sources, including heat registers, windows, doors and air conditioners. Damage varies depending on the plant and its vulnerabilities.

Control: Remove the plant from the drafty location.

FUNGUS GNATS

Fungus gnats are common across the country; every plant can be a host. These tiny, black flying insects flit and fly around your face and are often confused with fruit flies. Fruit flies are slightly larger and brownish-red. Adult fungus gnats are annoying but relatively harmless. However, the tiny, white, grub-like larvae may feed on young roots. Adults are attracted to fungus growing in moist or wet compost or potting mix.

Control: Allow the surface of the potting mix to dry slightly between waterings. Once the surface dries, the gnats' food source disappears. It can take days or weeks to be completely rid of them, or they may die off all on their own.

LEAF SPOT

Leaf spot can be caused by many things, including fungi, bacteria and insects. Tiny black specks are sometimes an indication of fungal damage. Leaf spot without the specks may indicate a bacterial problem.

Control: Remove the affected foliage and stems, and increase ventilation. Disinfect cutting tools with rubbing alcohol or bleach between cuts to prevent spreading the problem to healthy parts of the plant.

MEALYBUGS

Mealybugs are relatively common and easy to control. Slightly larger than most house-plant insects, they are oval, bright white and sometimes covered in a white, waxy substance that resembles cottony fluff. They move only if disturbed and crawl very slowly, leaving a sticky honeydew behind that can lead to sooty mold. Mealybugs are found individually or in large clusters on stems, undersides of leaves and where the leaf joins the stem. The damage results in weakened plant parts that eventually yellow and die.

Control: Spraying insecticides isn't always effective because the mealybugs' waxy surface repels liquids. Pyrethrum-based sprays are safe and effective if you can make good contact. Touching the bugs with a cotton swab dipped in rubbing alcohol is also effective. Rinse the plant under the tap while gently removing the bugs with your fingers works, or squish them.

POWDERY MILDEW

Powdery mildew is a fungal disease that appears on the surface of the foliage as a white, powdery coating. It won't kill the plant, but it will cause damage, including disfigured flowers and foliage. Not unlike other fungal-based problems, it occurs most often in locations with poor air circulation and high humidity. It can spread rapidly.

Control: Improve air circulation and remove infected portions of the plant. Treat the foliage with a mix of baking soda and water or a safe, non-toxic fungicide registered for use indoors.

RED SPIDER MITES

Red spider mites are very common, especially in drier climates. They are tiny, sap-sucking pests that are difficult to see with the naked eye. They're often discovered long after their arrival, when the damage is evident and their silky webbing is visible. Only then will you notice the tiny creatures moving to and fro. They congregate on the undersides of the leaves where the leaves join the stems and often on the newest of growth. They're especially fond of heat and dry air. The damage results in fine, yellow speckles on the foliage as it appears to fade and wither.

Control: Rinse susceptible plants regularly under tepid water. Gently massage the affected parts under the water, removing the webbing, residue and mites. Treat with pyrethrum sprays or insecticidal soap.

ROT

Rot is almost always caused by overwatering. One major sign of rot is foliage collapsing without any other signs of distress. A wilty plant that appears to be lacking moisture but that is sitting in moist potting mix is a sure sign of both root rot and crown or stem rot.

Control: Difficult. Once the rot has set in, the damage is irreversible. The best solution is prevention; try not to overwater your plants.

SCALE INSECTS

Scale insects are small and attach themselves to the undersides of leaves and along the stems. They suck the sap from the plant, weakening it. Over time, they also emit a sticky honeydew. Adults are immobile and reside under a protective, brown disc-like covering that repels insecticidal sprays. Nymphs can move from plant to plant.

Control: If discovered early enough, gently scrape them off with a fingernail, a soft, soapy toothbrush or a cotton swab dipped in rubbing alcohol. If discovered too late, they are more difficult to eradicate and it's best just to throw the plant away.

SOOTY MOLD

Sooty mold is a black fungus that grows on the sticky honeydew produced by a number of pests. The result is stunted and reduced growth.

Control: Treat pest problems immediately to reduce the chance of mold forming. Wipe the foliage with a damp cloth and rinse debris away.

THRIPS

Thrips are tiny, black insects that move very quickly. The wingless nymphs are pale, whereas adults have hairy wings and are darker. At different stages they can jump or fly from plant to plant. They leave silver streaks and black dots of excrement on the leaves where they scrape the tissue in order to suck the sap. The flowers can also become spotted and deformed.

Control: Remove all infected parts of the plant. If overall damage is too severe, discard the entire plant. Pyrethrum sprays are effective.

VIRUSES

Viruses can be complicated and are either misdiagnosed, confused with something else or discovered too late. Watch for stunted or distorted growth, streaked petals and irregular yellow blotches on the leaves. Viruses are often carried by sucking insects, infected tools and even your fingers.

Control: Once you or an expert has determined that the problem is viral, often all you can do is destroy the plant. Prevention is difficult.

WHITEFLY

Whitefly are tiny, white flying insects that are easy to spot. They can devaste a collection of plants. They can be difficult to eradicate completely because of their ability to move quickly and easily from plant to plant. They often hide under the foliage, where they lay their eggs. They multiply rapidly and rise up from the plant in a cloud when disturbed. These sap suckers deposit a layer of sticky honeydew on lower leaves as they feed.

Control: Yellow sticky traps will reduce the numbers somewhat, but you'll also need to apply an insecticidal soap or a pyrethrum-based spray. Treat late in the day or evening because they're more apt to fly away if treated during the day. Isolate the infested plant to prevent the spread of whitefly.

The HOUSE PLANTS

Aeonium

Aeonium

Features: interesting foliage and growth habit
Height: 12–36" (30–91 cm)
Spread: 12–18" (30–46 cm)

*Some stems form a solitary rosette
while others produce a colony.*

One of aeonium's most arresting features is its tightly packed, leafy rosettes. This plant is available with yellow, green, brown or almost black foliage, and when mature it produces bright yellow panicles of flowers. Once a stem has flowered, it soon dies.

Growing

Aeonium grows best in **bright light** year round. These plants prefer to grow in a **soil-based mix** with added **coarse sand** or **perlite**. This mix should remain **moist** during the growing season but allowed to dry out slightly between watering in winter. Ideal minimum temperatures are 50° F/10° C in winter and 75° F/24° C throughout the rest of the year. Apply a weak fertilizer every two weeks during the growth cycle. Let the plant rest during winter.

Tips

Good light is crucial for strong growth. Lack of light will result in sparse rosettes and elongated leaves that fall prematurely. Larger plants may require support or staking. Repot and propagate by seed, leaf or stem cuttings in spring. Grow aeonium in terra-cotta or ceramic pots rather than plastic to provide a stable base for the top-heavy stems and rosettes. Remove the stem that supported the flower once the flower has died.

Recommended

A. arboreum (saucer plant) is sparsely branched and grows slowly to 36" (91 cm) tall. The leaves, displayed in a rosette form, are semi-glossy and a little leathery to the touch. The foliage is usually green with purple to brown lines, usually on each leaf margin and midrib. **'Atropurpureum'** (purple tree aeonium, black plant) grows to the same height as the species, with freely branching, woody stems. Dark, glossy, purple leaves differentiate this variety from the species. **'Schwartzkopf'** has nearly black foliage.

All photos: *A. arboreum* 'Atropurpureum'

African Violet

Saintpaulia

Features: colorful flowers and fuzzy foliage **Height:** 1–8" (2.5–20 cm)
Spread: 2–8" (5.1–20 cm)

Over 30,000 varieties of African violet are available to enthusiasts and collectors, and it is considered the most popular houseplant in the world. African violets have been present in North American homes since the 1920s, 30 years after *S. ionantha*, the original species, was discovered in east Africa. Two of the chief assets of the African violet are that it's colorful and it's easy to grow, which may explain its enduring popularity.

Growing

African violets require **bright, indirect light** to thrive. To lengthen the blooming cycle, artificial light can be used to supplement natural light during winter. Use a minimum of 5000 lux for 12 or more hours a day (see lighting section page 22). Plant in **well-drained compost** and keep **consistently moist**, but allow the surface to dry slightly between waterings. An extreme increase or decrease in temperature can damage and even kill the plant.

Tips

African violets are best grown in plastic rather than terra-cotta pots. Plastic is easier to clean and disinfect, and terra-cotta tends to dry the compost more readily and maintains a high salt content. Small pots should be watered from the bottom by immersing the pot in a saucer of tepid water, but larger pots should be watered from the top, under the foliage. Avoid wetting the leaves, which may cause spotting, mildew or rot. African violets prefer to be slightly pot-bound. Deadhead flowers, including flowerless stems, from the base. Increase humidity by placing pots on pebble trays. To propagate, take stem cuttings or sow seeds in spring.

Recommended

The species is not usually available, but current hybrids offer a variety of sizes, leaf types and flower forms and colors. African violets are grouped according to the maximum width of the mature plant. The groupings include micro-miniature (less than 3"/8 cm), miniature (3–6"/8–15 cm), semi-miniature (6–8"/15–20 cm); standard (8–16"/20–40 cm) and large (over 16"/40 cm).

Deadhead regularly and remove the entire flower stalk once the cluster has faded.

Above: 'Coral Crunch'

Trailing varieties, which are determined by a minimum of three crowns, long drooping stems and smaller flowers than the standard, are available in each group.

Saintpaulia spp. plants usually produce a low-growing rosette of fuzzy leaves on red-tinged, hairy stems. The leaves and stems are fleshy and tender. Flower stalks emerge from the plant's crown, tipped with star- or violet-shaped flowers with a pronounced yellow center. The flowers often sit above the foliage and are borne singly or in clusters. The flowers can be single, semi-double and double in form with smooth or frilly edges. They are available in white, purple, pink, blue, red and every shade between. Petals can be solid or

Microminiature variety

Below: 'Powder Keg' with white picotee edging

bicolor, striped or patterned, tiny or large. Hundreds of cultivars have been bred from the species, and new varieties are available from one year to the next. Some varieties have variegated foliage, but these are difficult to find.

Problems & Pests

Aphids, leaf and bud eelworms, mealybugs, root mealybugs, gray mold, fungus and bacteria problems, powdery mildew

Above: 'Rob's Boondoggle'

When forcing African violets for periods longer than one to two months, allow the plant to rest for at least one month annually.

Center: 'Raphael'

Aloe

Aloe

Features: succulent foliage and flower spike **Height:** 12–24" (30–61 cm)
Spread: 24–36" (30–91 cm)

Aloes are slow-growing succulents with thick, tentacle-like leaves edged with hooked teeth. The most well-known aloe plant is *Aloe vera*, but it's not alone. A number of other aloes closely resemble the most common species, and they grow in a variety of patterns, sizes and shapes. *A. vera* flowers infrequently indoors, but when it does, it bears a tall, green stalk topped with a cluster of long flowers in yellow to soft pink. Aloe is easy to grow and will thrive on a sunny windowsill in almost any home environment.

Growing

Aloe plants prefer a **bright** location with **a little direct sunlight** in winter. They grow best in a **soil-based mix** with added **coarse sand** to ensure adequate drainage. Allow the soil to almost dry out between waterings. Water approximately once a month during winter. Feed monthly from spring to fall with a fertilizer high in potash. Aloe tolerates dry air but prefers average humidity.

Above: *A. aristata*

Tips

Water by immersing the pot for ten minutes to thoroughly soak the root ball. If watering from above, do not allow water to collect where the leaves emerge or they will rot from the base. Repot annually in spring if necessary; propagate offsets when the leaves begin to form rosettes.

Recommended

A. aristata (lace aloe, guinea-fowl aloe) forms a tight ball of dark leaves covered with raised white spots and edged with soft ivory spines. It bears orange-red flowers.

A. humilis (spider aloe, crocodile jaws) bears upright, 4–6" (10–15 cm) long, spiny, bluish green leaves that curve inwards. The leaves are covered in creamy white bumps. Red flowers are tipped in ocher. 'Globosa' is slightly smaller with blue-tinged leaves.

A. jucunda (hedgehog aloe) forms a cluster of tiny rosettes made up of dark, green, spiny leaves with creamy blotches. A single flower spike of pale pink and white flowers emerges from the center of each rosette, which grows 3" (7.6 cm) tall and wide.

A. variegata (partridge-breast aloe, tiger aloe) is a dwarf plant with tight, spiraling rosettes of smooth-edged leaves. The leaves are 6" (15 cm) long and 1–2" (2.5–5 cm) wide with irregular, paler bands of green. Coral pink flowers are borne atop 12" stems from each rosette.

A. vera (*A. barbadensis*, medicine aloe) bears a stemless clump of thick, grayish green, pointed leaves edged with soft teeth. The leaves are 12–24" (30–61 cm) long and 2–3" (5–7.6 cm) wide and covered in smooth spots that fade with age. Drooping, tubular, yellow flowers are carried on 36" (91 cm) tall green stalk. *A. vera* is considered medicinal.

Problems & Pests

Scale insects, mealybugs and root mealybugs

The sap in A. vera *leaves has amazing curative qualities when rubbed on burns, cuts, abrasions and bruises.*

Inset opposite: tall flower spike

Angel Wings

Caladium

Features: colorful, ornate foliage **Height:** 12–24" (30–61 cm)
Spread: 12–24" (30–61 cm)

Angel wings requires a little more care than a typical houseplant because it is a summer bulb (tuber), but the results are well worth it. The foliage is dazzling from the minute it emerges—papery thin, arrow-shaped leaves mottled and veined with pinks, reds, greens and whites. Three groups of angel wings are available, including fancy-leaf and strap-leaf varieties. Perhaps the only downfall of this plant is that its brilliant foliage dies in fall and the tuber remains dormant until spring.

Growing

Angel wings grows best in **bright to moderate, indirect sunlight.** Use a **well-drained, soil-less mix** and keep it **moderately moist** during the growing season. Do not water during dormancy; water only after new sprouts begin to emerge. Angel wings prefers warm to normal temperatures and high to moderate humidity. Supplement humidity by misting the leaves regularly in spring.

Above: 'Florida Sweetheart'

Tips

Once dormant, the tuber can be left in the pot or removed and stored in dry peat moss at about 60° F/15° C. To break dormancy and encourage growth, plant the tuber about 1–2" (2.5–5.1 cm) deep with sprouts facing upward for large leaves or upside down for smaller, more abundant leaves. Keep the pot in a warm area for at least three weeks. Once the tubers have sprouted, mist daily and relocate to a bright area to encourage leaf color. The small offsets or small tubers can be potted separately in spring as well. Remove flowers as they emerge.

Recommended

C. bicolor (*C. x hortulanum*) bears paper thin, heart-shaped leaves on long, arching stalks. The multicolored leaves are available in many combinations of pink, white, gold, green and crimson. Insignificant arum-like flowers may occur.

Fancy-leaf angel wings usually have large leaves, grow 18–24" (46–61 cm) tall and prefer filtered shade or afternoon shade and morning sun. This group includes varieties

such as '**Carolyn Whorton**,' which bears pink leaves with dark green marbling and red ribs; '**Pink Beauty**,' which has green and pink marbled leaves along red ribs; and '**Rosabud**,' which sports leaves with a pink-center surrounded by white and green, and tricolored ribs. Strap-leaf varieties produce elongated, narrow, heart-shaped leaves that tolerate sun all day. They generally grow 12–14" (30–36 cm) tall and are useful in hanging baskets. This group includes varieties such as '**Candidum Jr.**,' which has white leaves with dark green veins and edges; '**Miss Muffet**,' which bears dwarf, sage green leaves with white ribs; and '**Red Frill**,' whose red-shaded leaves have green margins.

Problems & Pests

Aphids and red spider mites

Opposite: 'Pink Beauty'
Right: 'White Queen'

Arrowhead Vine

Syngonium

Features: patterned foliage and bushy form **Height:** 8"–4' (20 cm–1.2 m)
Spread: 8"–4' (20 cm–1.2 m)

*Arrowhead vine is also commonly
known as goosefoot plant.*

It's not surprising that this plant is commonly known as arrowhead vine. Each leaf emerges as a simple arrowhead shape, but over time transforms itself into a deeply lobed leaf made up of five leaflets. There is no end to the possible variations of leaf patterns and shapes, which can vary even on the same plant. The leaves, however, come only in shades of white, cream and green.

Above: 'Emerald Gem'

Growing

Variegated types of arrowhead vine prefer **bright light** with no direct sunlight whereas solid green types prefer **partial shade**. The **peat moss** or **soil-based mix** with added **peat moss** should be kept **evenly moist** in summer. Allow the surface to dry out between waterings. Water less frequently in winter, and let the top half of the potting mix dry out between waterings. Arrowhead vine requires normal room temperatures, with a winter minimum temperature of 60° F/16° C. Mist regularly or supplement humidity with a pebble tray.

Tips

Arrowhead vine is a climber, so support may be necessary over time if you choose to train it vertically. The aerial roots that emerge from the stems can be encouraged to grow into a moss pole. Arrowhead vine can also be allowed to trail naturally over the edges of a pot. A bushy form and juvenile foliage can be maintained by removing any climbing stems once they begin to form. Propagate by using cuttings of stem sections with aerial roots in spring or summer. • All parts of arrowhead vine are poisonous if ingested.

Opposite & right: *S. podophyllum*

Recommended

S. podophyllum is a small, compact plant when young, but it spreads into a trailing or climbing form as it matures. The younger leaves often have silvery white veining or blotchy white or creamy variegations. The leaf shape changes over time, resulting in a deeply lobed leaf composed of five leaflets. Arum-like, white, green or purple flowers are rarely produced and only on adult plants. '**Butterfly**' has deep green leaves with lighter colored veins. '**Emerald Gem**' has creamy white veins and margins on a green base. '**Green Gold**' leaves have white centers and a central margin with green along the edge. '**Imperial White**' has white marbled leaves, and '**Pixie**' is a compact, small-leaved form.

Problems & Pests

Mealybugs, scale insects, aphids and red spider mites

Asparagus Fern

Asparagus

Features: fern-like foliage and growth habit **Height:** 36" (91 cm)
Spread: 36" (91 cm)

Asparagus fern is, in fact, not a fern at all. Unlike a true fern, asparagus fern produces flowers, although they are insignificant in appearance. Asparagus fern is also adaptable to a wider range of conditions and is easier to grow than most true ferns. This plant is a relative of the lily, so it's not surprising that it produces fleshy roots often with pronounced tubers. The fleshy roots store water, which allows the plant to survive periods of dryness or neglect. Its most outstanding and unique feature is its finely divided, needle-like foliage, which resembles fern leaves, hence its common name. The leaves aren't leaves at all, but modified stems or branches.

Inset: *A. plumosus;* below: *A. densiflorus* 'Sprengeri'

Growing

Asparagus fern grows best in **bright, filtered sun**. Avoid deep shade and direct sunlight. Keep the **soil-based mix evenly moist**, but allow the surface to dry out a little between watering, and water less during winter. Mist occasionally to supplement the humidity levels. This plant prefers normal room temperatures, with a winter minimum temperature of 45°–50° F/7°–10° C. *A. setaceus* won't tolerate winter temperatures of less than 55° F/13° C.

Above: *A. densiflorus* 'Myers'

Tips

Repot and propagate annually in spring. Leave enough space from the pot's rim to allow the thick, tuberous roots to force the soil up as they grow. Propagate by dividing old, overcrowded clumps that have lost their vigor. Try to retain as many of the roots as possible. Asparagus fern is ideal for hanging baskets or in a location where the stems can cascade freely. • The berries are poisonous if ingested and contact with sap from stems and foliage can irritate skin.

Recommended

A. asparagoides (smilax) is a vigorous grower with trailing stems that grow 5' (1.7 m) long or more.

A. densiflorus 'Myers' (foxtail fern, plume asparagus) bears needle-like branchlets neatly arranged on stems resembling spikes. The stems are 15–18" (38–46 cm) long. 'Sprengeri' (emerald fern) has bright green, drooping stems covered in 1" (2.5 cm) long, needle-like foliage. It spreads to 36" (91 cm). Inconspicuous, whitish pink flowers are produced on arching stems, followed by reddish berries.

A. falcatus (siklethorn) has large, narrow, prickly leaves on 36" (91 cm) tall stems.

A. setaceus (*A. plumosus*, asparagus fern) is a compact plant with graceful, spreading branches that feature wispy foliage when young. The stems become a little straggly with age. On mature plants, berries sometimes follow after insignifcant flowers. 'Nanus' is slightly smaller than the species.

Problems & Pests

Scale insects and red spider mites may attack if humidity levels are too low.

Florists frequently use smilax *for fresh arrangements.*

Below: *A. densiflorus* 'Sprengeri'

Baby's Tears

Soleirolia

Features: thick mat of tiny leaves **Height:** 2" (5.1 cm) **Length:** trailing stems can reach 24" (61 cm) **Spread:** 1–2" (2.5–5.1 cm) wider than the container

This plant is also known as pollyanna vine, angel's tears, Irish moss, Corsican curse, and its botanical name was formerly Helxine soleirolii.

Baby's tears is also known as mind-your-own-business. No, you read it correctly. It's an odd but apropos name only because this creeping evergreen can become a bit of a weed in its native habitat and in terrariums. It may have an invasive reputation, but it is as cute as a button! The tiny, rounded leaves are carried on delicate, thin stems. A thick mat will eventually cover the perimeter of a pot and trail over the sides. This plant is easy to care for and is especially attractive when planted in a terrarium, around the base of other, larger plant specimens and in hanging baskets.

Growing

Baby's tears prefers **bright, filtered light**. The **soil-based mix** should be **moist** at all times. If it is allowed to dry out completely, the plant's thin stems will be damaged beyond repair. Mist frequently to supplement humidity levels. Rooms with average warmth are best, with a minimum winter temperature of 45° F/7° C.

Tips

Baby's tears looks great in terrariums, but make sure to keep the plant under control. Remove any rooting stems from areas you'd like to remain unplanted, and trim when necessary. Propagation is easy because of its natural tendency to root with little effort. Simply divide the rootball into clumps and place on the surface of moist potting mix in a pot. The stems will root in a short span of time. Repot if necessary in spring.

All photos: S. soleirolii

Recommended

S. soleirolii produces a thick mat of tiny leaves carried alternately on thin, fragile stems. This creeping species is solid green while **'Aurea'** is pale yellow and **'Variegata'** is silver.

Begonia

Begonia

Features: showy flowers and foliage **Height:** 4–24" (10–61 cm)
Spread: 4–24" (10–61 cm)

Begonias have a few common characteristics. There are begonias grown strictly for their foliage and others grown just for their flowers. There are three groups made up of approximately 1000–2000 begonia hybrids, which range in size from plants small enough to grow in the palm of your hand, to others that could easily obscure a conservatory wall. Begonia flowers are either male or female and borne in clusters; the stems are often fleshy and the leaves mostly lop-sided. Some are better candidates than others for the home, and that's where we begin. Rex begonias are my personal favorite simply because their foliage is like a work of art, and they're easy to maintain.

Growing

Begonias prefer **moderate to bright, filtered light** with no direct sunlight. They'll grow equally well in a **soil-less** or **soil-based mix.** Keep **evenly moist,** but allow the mix to dry out slightly between waterings. Withhold water from those that die back during a rest period or dormancy once the foliage begins to yellow. Humidity levels should be high, but avoid spraying water directly onto the leaves. Normal room temperatures are sufficient, but maintain a winter temperature of 60° F/16° C.

Begonias are sensitive to over- and underwatering.

Opposite & right:
B. rex cultivars

Above: *B. masoniana*

Tips

Many begonias are prone to mildew, so provide adequate air circulation and pick off infected leaves immediately. Deadhead the flowers regularly. Apply a weak fertilizer while in bud and during the flowering cycle. Propagate by division, leaf cuttings and seed. • The rhizomes are poisonous if ingested.

Below: *B. rex* cultivar

Recommended

The following are a few begonias that I recommend for the beginner.

B. 'Cleopatra' (mapleleaf begonia) is a small, bushy plant that grows 6–9" (15–23 cm) tall. It produces glistening bronze leaves with hairy undersides and splashes of brown on the upper sides.

B. imperialis has toothed, light green leaves with silver splashes along the main veins. The upper surfaces are bumpy and covered with fine hairs. It bears sparse, white flowers and grows to 5" (13 cm) tall and 9" (23 cm) wide.

B. maculata has cane-like stems that grow very tall, supporting 9" (23 cm) long leaves. Both sides of the leaves are spotted white.

B. masoniana (iron cross begonia) has large, bright green, puckered leaves with a central mahogany red cross and insignificant flowers.

B. rex (rex begonia) isn't commonly found, but its hybrids are. The deeply textured leaves are generally asymmetrical, up to 9" (23 cm) long and brightly variegated. The colors include green, silver, brown, red, pink and purple. 'Bettina Rothschild' has green leaves with maroon central margins, veins, stems and edges, 'Her Majesty' has bronzy brown center and outer edges with creamy white variegations, and 'Merry Christmas' has a burgundy center, surrounded by gold, then green and edged in maroon.

B. sutherlandii is a trailing begonia with small lance-shaped leaves with red edges. It bears a profusion of single, salmon flowers in loose, pendulous clusters. It grows 6–8" (15–20 cm) tall.

Problems & Pests

Mealybugs, red spider mites, thrips, whiteflies, powdery mildew, stem rot and gray mold can all become problems if begonias are grown without the right care or in the wrong location.

All begonias suffer in dry air. Humidity can be supplemented with pebble trays.

Above: *B. rex* cultiva; below: *B. sutherlandii*

Bridal Veil

Gibasis

Features: trailing habit, purple and green foliage and tiny white flowers
Height: 4–6" (10–14 cm) tall **Length:** trailing stems can grow 36" (91 cm)
long or more **Spread:** 6–8" (15–20 cm) wider than container

Bridal veil is loved by some and loathed by others. I love this plant and
have two specimens to prove it. They can become untidy looking, but
with a little trimming and some time spent outdoors in summer, they
become lush and full once again.

Related to silvery inch plant (*Trades-cantia*), this creeper greatly resembles
its relative. The two species are often confused with one another because
they look so similar. Bridal veil is frequently sold in hanging baskets and is
very easy to care for.

Inset: *G. geniculata*

Growing

Bridal veil requires **bright light with a short period of direct sunlight.** Keep the **soil-based mix consistently moist,** but allow it to dry out slightly between waterings in winter. Mist occasionally and repot every two years if necessary. Bridal veil prefers average to warm room temperatures, with a minimum winter temperature of 45° F/7° C.

Tips

Propagate by division or stem cuttings, and repot in spring if necessary. Trim the trailing stems back by one-third to half annually, or more often if necessary to allow the center to fill back out rather than expending energy on long trailers. Bridal veil also benefits from being outdoors in a moderately lit space throughout summer.

Recommended

G. geniculata (Tahitian bridal veil) produces trailing stems that carry dark green leaves alternately from stem to tip. The undersides are purple and both sides are sparsely hairy. Tiny, white flowers are borne atop the dark foliage sporadically throughout the year.

G. pellucida (dotted bridal veil, bridal veil) is almost identical in appearance and habit to *G. geniculata*, so the two species are often confused with one another. *G. pellucida* has has a more delicate appearance, slightly smaller leaves and grows to two-thirds the size of *G. geniculata.*

Problems & Pests

Aphids and red spider mites can occur, but infrequently.

G. pellucida *is native to parts of* Mexico *while* G. geniculata *is native to Paraguay, Argentina and Mexico.*

This page & left bottom: *G. pellucida*

Bromeliad

Aechmea, Billbergia, Cryptanthus, Guzmania,
Neoregelia, Tillandsia

Features: showy foliage and exotic, colorful flowers **Height:** 7–36" (18–91 cm)
Spread: 7–36" (18–91 cm)

Bromeliads are a group consisting of 2700 species in more than 56 genera.
They include three types: terrestrial, saxicolous and epiphytic. Terrestrial
bromeliads draw moisture and nutrients from the soil through normal root
systems. Saxicolous bromeliads are found growing on rocks in their native
habitat, drawing moisture and nutrients from cracks and fissures on rocky
outcrops. Both terrestrial and saxicolous bromeliads can be grown in pots.
Epiphytic bromeliads, sometimes known as air plants, take moisture from
the air and nutrients from fallen debris and dust. Their
roots provide support, anchoring the plant to its host.
This group belongs to the genus *Tillandsia* and includes
both green- and gray-leaved species. Both can adapt to
being grown in a pot, but the gray-leaved species are better mounted on a vertical or horizontal surface. Bromeliads are fascinating plants suitable for growing indoors.
They're relatively easy to grow and can be a great learning tool for children and adults.

Inset: *Cryptanthus bromelioides* 'Tricolor'

Growing

Most bromeliads grow well in **bright, filtered** or **bright, indirect sunlight**. A **well-drained, light potting medium** is essential when growing bromeliads in pots. They should remain **consistently moist** without completely drying out or becoming waterlogged. The central vase or urn of each 'rosette' should remain full of water at all times. Potting mixes vary for each group. Terrestrial and saxicolous bromeliads require a basic mix of one part shredded peat or coir, one part screened garden compost or leaf mold and three parts sharp gritty sand or crushed granite chippings. When grown in pots, epiphytes will grow happily in a commercial orchid mix amended with gritty sand. Other combinations can be made up of bark chips or mulch, coir, perlite, horticultural charcoal, grit, peat moss and sphagnum moss. They cannot tolerate temperatures cooler than 55° F/13° C and require at least 75° F/24° C to flower.

Tips

Bromeliads can grow in or on a number of things, including terrariums, pots, slabs of bark or decorative items such as shells and mirrors, depending on which group the bromeliad falls into. They thrive outside during spring and summer, particularly in mild climates. Propagating bromeliads is done simply by removing the offsets or pups at their base once they've reached at least one-third of the original plant's size. The offsets should be planted in a rich, moist potting mix.

This page & left bottom: *Guzmania lingulata*

Above: *Neoregelia carolinae* 'Tricolor'

All parts of any bromeliad are poisonous if ingested, and handling may cause skin irritation.

Recommended

Aechmea fasciata (silver vase) is an epiphytic bromeliad best grown in a pot. Leathery, silver-banded, gray-green leaves can reach 24–36" (61–91 cm) tall

and wide. A rosette form results from a distinct central 'vase' from which a flower stalk will emerge with tiny blue flowers tucked between bright pink bracts. Other cultivars have solid silver to cream-striped variegations.

Billbergia nutans (queen's tears) grows to 12" (30 cm) tall and bears narrow, strap-like, arching foliage. Flowers dangle from arching bright pink bracts on tall, central stalks. This species is an epiphyte.

Cryptanthus bibittatus (earth star) is a terrestrial bromeliad that forms a 7–10" (18–25 cm) tall and wide rosette of spiny-edged foliage. Striped, dark brownish green leaves become tinged with pink in stronger light. Small, inconspicuous flowers emerge from the center.

Guzmania lingulata (scarlet star) is an epiphyte with smooth, glossy, strap-like leaves that grow to 18" (46 cm) long. White flowers emerge from the central scarlet, star-shaped bracts.

Neoregelia carolinae (blushing bromeliad) is a terrestrial bromeliad that grows to 15–25" (38–64 cm) tall and wide. The foliage is striped with white variegations that emerge from a bright pink center. The 'blushing' center turns reddish purple when flowering. Short, stocky, bright red bracts emerge from the center. '**Tricolor**' also has creamy yellow, striped leaves that turn pink as they mature.

Tillandsia cyanea (pink quill, blue flowered torch) is an epiphytic bromeliad that grows 12" (30 cm) tall and wide. Green, grass-like leaves surround a tall stalk supporting blue-purple flowers held between bright pink bracts. Gray *Tillandsia* closely resembles its green counterpart and is more commonly known as air plant. The leaves of air plant are covered in furry scales for nutrient and water absorption. They're easily mounted on just about any hard surface.

Problems & Pests
Aphids, scale insects, red spider mites and mealybugs

Buddhist Pine

Podocarpus

Features: grass-like foliage,
upright and bushy growth habit
Height: 6' (1.8 m)
Spread: 36" (91 cm)

The Buddhist pine is also known as Japanese yew or Kusamaki, a reference to where it's found. This slow-growing conifer can reach 60' (18 m) in its native habitat but remains smaller when forced to grow in a container. It can be kept even more compact by regular pruning. It's imperative that Buddhist pine be grown in a cool location indoors. It tolerates drafts, making it ideal for a hallway or foyer. Older specimens are easily recognizable because they display natural characteristics similar to those of a bonsai-pruned plant. They're elegant, graceful and a must for any plant collector.

Growing

Buddhist pines prefer **bright, filtered light to partial shade.** Keep the **soil– or peat moss–based mix moist** from spring to fall, but water less in winter. Mist regularly during periods of hot weather. Cool to normal room temperatures are fine, with a minimum winter temperature of 40° F/4° C.

Tips

Propagate by sowing seeds or stem cuttings in late spring or summer. The fleshy seeds resemble fruits but are rarely present because it's highly unlikely that Buddhist pine would ever flower indoors. • The fruit-like seeds are poisonous if ingested.

Recommended

P. macrophyllus is an upright tree with a dense columnar form. The older stems are covered in a reddish brown bark. Narrow, almost grass-like leaves run the length of each stem from the base to the tip. It produces inconspicuous flowers followed by seeds that resemble red berries, but rarely does so when grown in a pot. '**Maki**' is slightly more narrow and upright than the species. The growth is more compact with shorter leaves.

Problems & Pests

Red spider mites can occur, but only in dry and hot conditions.

All photos: *P. macrophyllus*

Cacti & Succulents

Cacti: *Aprorocactus, Cephalocereus, Echinocactus, Epiphyllum, Gymnocalycium, Opuntia, Schlumbergera*
Succulents: *Echeveria, Euphorbia, Faucacia, Haworthia, Sedum*

Features: form, spines and flowers **Height:** varies **Spread:** varies

Cacti are fascinating. While there are many to choose from in every shape, color and size imaginable, generally all cacti can be divided into two types: the desert (or terrestrial) cactus and the forest (or epiphytic) cactus. The majority of the spiny varieties available are desert cacti. Most often, they're well armed and produce exotic, brightly colored flowers. Forest cacti, or epiphytes, include the familiar Christmas cactus and are native to woodlands and jungles rather than the arid regions that the desert types call home. Generally, forest types have flat, stemlike leaves without spines. They are grown for their flowers, which emerge sometime in December with a little encouragement. All cacti are strange and wonderful, a world apart from all other plants.

Inset: *Opuntia* spp.

Cacti

Growing

Both cactus types require as much **bright light** daily as possible. Desert type cacti can tolerate periods of direct sun, but forest type cacti should be shaded from direct sunlight. **Desert type cacti** prefer to be **watered thoroughly** when the mix begins to dry out from spring to late summer. Keep almost dry, watering only enough to prevent shriveling from late summer to mid-spring. Water **forest type cacti** as you would an ordinary houseplant during active growth and when flowers appear. Decrease watering during the winter rest period. Only forest type cacti require higher humidity, so mist the leaves frequently. Desert type cactus prefer average warmth from spring to fall and a minimum winter temperature of 50°–55° F/10°–12° C. Forest type cactus prefer 55°–70° F/12°–21° C while actively growing and 50°–55° F/10°–12° C during their rest period.

Tips

Repot cacti when young, but later repot only when necessary because a small pot will encourage flowering. To prevent injury when repotting, wrap a strip of folded newspaper around a prickly cactus before removing it from the pot. Cacti aren't very effective as specimens but are striking in groups. They're often displayed in cactus gardens unless they're very large.

Not all cacti will flower when young, but the following do: Echinopsis, Lobivia, Mammalaria, Notocactus, Parodia *and* Rebuta.

Recommended

Desert type cactus: A large variety of cacti are available in this group, but I'll only touch upon a few, based mostly on their shape.

Aprorocactus flagelliformis (rat's tail cactus) produces 1/2" (1.25 cm) wide, tubular

stems covered in spiny barbs and can reach 36" (7.6 cm) or more in height. Bright pink, tubular flowers bloom for up to two months, but the individual flowers last for only a week. Rat's tail cactus is best displayed in a hanging basket.

Columnar varieties are striking specimens when mature. Most interesting is *Cephalocereus senilis* (old man cactus) because of the fine white hairs that almost totally obscure the columnar body and sharp spines.

One of the more popular globular cacti available is *Echinocactus grusonii* (barrel cactus). It forms a perfectly round, ribbed ball covered in rigid, extremely sharp spines. The yellowish spines run along each rib edge from top to bottom. This slow-growing ball will grow to a 9" (23 cm) diameter but will take 10 or more years to reach that size.

Grafted cacti are becoming more popular and offer color without flowers. *Gymnocalycium mihanovichii friedrichii* (Hibotan cactus) is a two-part cactus. The colorful cap lacks chlorophyll, which results in its brilliant colors. The bottom supporting half is that of another genus. Some grafted cacti flower but others do not.

Below: *Echinocactus grusonii*

Branched or pad-like cacti are unique, too. *Opuntia microdasys* (bunny ears) has flattish, succulent pads covered in spiny polka dots. New pads emerge from existing pads on top of one another. The spines can vary on this type of cactus, from fuzzy dots to long, needle-like spines.

Forest type cactus: *Epiphyllum acher-manii* (orchid cactus) is a member of this group. The stems sprawl outwards and support the multi-layered, brightly colored flowers in shades of red, orange, white, purple, yellow and pink. This group also includes such genera as the familiar *Schlumbergera* x *buckleyi* (Christmas cactus) and *Schlumbergera truncata* (crab cactus). They both have sectioned, flattish leaves that arch in a trailing form when mature. Bright, trumpet-shaped, pink- or red-layered flowers emerge from the tips of the newest growth.

Succulents

Simply defined, succulents are plants without leaves or with thick or fleshy leaves and/or stems that are capable of storing water. They often lack modified spines or hairs. Succulents come in a huge variety of shapes, sizes and forms. Their growth habit tends to be a tightly packed rosette form, ideal for conserving

Above: *Euphorbia tirucalli*

moisture in the arid habitats they usually call home. Some succulents display a tree-like habit while others are shrubby or trailing.

Above & top right: *Echeveria glauca*

Growing

Despite the great number of leaf forms and growth habits, all succulents need a **well-drained potting mix**, **bright sun**, **good air circulation**, **moisture** throughout the growing season and a slightly drier rest period soon after. Flowering succulents must have a rest period to thrive and bloom from year to year. All succulents love a vacation outdoors, in the right location, during the summer months.

Recommended

Echeveria glauca (blue echeveria) produces tightly packed rosettes of succulent, bright blue foliage.

Euphorbia tirucalli (milk bush, pencil euphorbia) is an interesting succulent. It produces thick, smooth, green, leafless stems in a free-branching, shrubby form. A fascinating globular euphorbia species known as **Turkish Temple** (*E. obesa*) is also available.

Faucaria tigrina (tiger jaws) produces fleshy leaves in a rosette form, with soft, spine-like teeth along each leaf edge. They produce bright yellow flowers in summer.

Cacti are very collectable. A modest-sized home can easily house hundreds of cacti at a time.

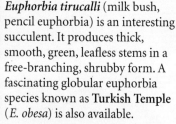

Haworthia fasciata (zebra hawor-thia) resembles an aloe or agave in form and bears thick, sharply pointed, ribbed foliage. A great number of *Haworthia* species are available in varied sizes, patterns and forms.

Sedum morganianum (donkey's tail, burro's tail) is a popular succu-lent. Its long, trailing stems of clus-tered, thick, bean-like leaves resemble the tail of a donkey. These stems can reach 24" (61 cm) lengths.

Problems & Pests
Mealybugs and rot

Combine tiny cactus and succulents in a shallow pot. Plant them closely together for impact and contrast.

Above left: *Faucaria tigrina*; right: *Haworthia fasciata*

Above: *Sedum morganianum*

Calamondin

x Citrofortunella

Features: fruit, flowers and bushy form
Height: 4' (1.2 m)
Spread: 24–36" (61–91 cm)

*Even young, barely rooted
cuttings often start to bloom
and produce fruit.*

The calamondin x *Citrofortunella* is a hybrid genus, a cross between the genus *Citrus*, mainly fruit trees, and the genus *Fortunella*, mainly evergreen trees and shrubs. The calamondin x *C. macrocarpa* is a cross between a tangerine and a kumquat, and the result is a popular indoor plant that produces yummy miniature oranges on a compact tree. Calamondin is an attractive specimen ideal for a sunny setting because it is both ornamental and functional. This is a fun plant for children to grow because there always seems to be something happening. It can flower and fruit in unison and even young cuttings will bear fruit.

Growing

Calamondin prefers **bright light** with **several hours of direct sunlight** daily. The **soil-less or acidic mix** should be kept **consistently moist,** but allow the surface of the potting mix to dry out slightly between waterings. It prefers moderate to high humidity, supplemented with misting or a pebble tray. Normal room temperatures are suitable, with a winter minimum temperature of 50° F/10° C.

Tips

Calamondin can be placed outside in summer after careful acclimatization. A fertilizer containing magnesium and iron will help compensate for its tendency to be deficient in these elements. Pollinate the flowers by dabbing the flowers' stamens with a small paintbrush. Propagate by cuttings or seeds in the spring.

All photos: x *C. microcarpa*

Recommended

x *Citrofortunella microcarpa* bears glossy, dark green foliage and small clusters of sweetly scented, star-shaped white flowers. Miniature orange fruits follow and mature to approximately 1^1/$_2$" (3.8 cm) across. The fruit is slightly bitter. The flowers usually appear in summer, but both the flowers and fruit may be produced almost year-round in the right conditions. 'Tiger' has leaves edged and streaked with white. 'Variegata' is a compact variety with mottled white and gray leaves and variegated green fruit that later turns a bright orange.

Problems & Pests

Scale insects and red spider mites may attack in dry conditions.

The fruit is ideal for making marmalade.

Calathea

Calathea

Features: colorful, intricately patterned foliage **Height:** 12–24" (30–61 cm)
Spread: 12–24" (30–61 cm)

Calathea plants are ornately patterned and offer color without relying upon flowers. There are many *Calathea* species and cultivars available in pink, purple, red, maroon and dark green to almost black, and in color com-

binations that some would consider to be garish, but I am drawn to them over and over again. These plants can be a little demanding and short lived unless provided with sufficient warmth and humidity. Calatheas do bear flowers, but they are small and asymmetrical, insignificant at best and not common in container-bound plants. The calathea's strikingly exotic foliage makes it a conversation piece anywhere it is displayed.

Inset: *C. ornata*

Growing

Calathea prefers **partial shade** with no direct sunlight. The **peat moss–** or **soil-based mix** should be kept **consistently moist** during the growing season, but water more sparingly in winter. Mist the foliage frequently, and keep the plant in an evenly warm location, with a minimum winter temperature of 60° F/16° C. Pebble trays are beneficial.

Tips

To prevent foliar damage, never allow the soil to dry out during the growing season. Repot and propagate by division annually, if necessary, in the spring.

Recommended

C. insignis (rattlesnake plant) produces spear-shaped leaves with purple undersides and wavy margins. The leaves are 18" (46 cm) long and lance-shaped with alternating small and large dark green blotches along each side of the main vein.

C. makoyana (peacock plant, cathedral windows) produces 12" (30 cm) long, upright, papery leaves on long stalks. The oval leaves are light green, with a fine, feather-like pattern of dark green lines running from the midrib to the leaf edge and irregularly shaped blotches occurring at intervals. The undersides are marked and maroon.

C. ornata is smaller and bears dark green leaves with thin pink veins that turn white with age and purple undersides.

C. roseopicta produces large, dark green, oval, 8" (20 cm) long leaves with dark purple stripes from the

C. zebrina

midrib to the leaf edge and a creamy white stripe that runs parallel to the leaf edge.

C. zebrina (zebra plant) produces 12" (30 cm) long, lance-shaped leaves with a velvety surface. The undersides are reddish purple and upper surfaces are marked with even green patches along the main vein.

Problems & Pests

Red spider mites, mealybugs and scale insects

Right: *C. roseopicta*

Cardboard Palm

Zamia

Features: stiff, unusual foliage, habit and low maintenance
Height: 4' (1.2 m) **Spread:** 4–6' (1.2 m–1.8 m)

Cardboard palm is native to Mexico and is often used as an outdoor landscape plant in subtropical and tropical regions worldwide.

Cardboard palm is one of those newly introduced houseplants that resembles plant life from millions of years ago, and there's good reason why. *Zamia* spp. have persevered for eons and were likely trampled by the odd dinosaur in primitive times. Cardboard palm is in fact not a palm at all, but an evergreen related to both Japanese sago palm and the ZZ plant. They all belong to the same family, *Cycadaceae*. This incredibly unique plant is another ideal specimen for the indoor environment, offering an exotic display for those with enough room for it to grow and mature. It requires little care or maintenance, can tolerate poor light conditions, little humidity and bouts of neglect. Cardboard palm is a great specimen for the beginner or the collector.

Growing

Cardboard palm prefers **bright light to partial shade**. The **well-drained, soil-based mix** should be kept **moderately moist** but allowed to dry slightly between waterings. Moderate to high humidity is best. Average room temperatures are best, with a minimum winter temperature of 50° F/ 10° C.

Tips

Cardboard palms make great specimens and accent plants in areas with little foot traffic and enough space. They are drought tolerant and tough enough to withstand occasional neglect and poor or harsh indoor spaces. Propagate by seed in a moist peat and sand mixture. Avoid placing the seedlings in direct sunlight because they may burn. Germination will occur at temperatures above 64° F/18° C. Cardboard palms are often killed by overwatering. • All parts are poisonous if ingested, but consuming the seeds can be deadly. Place the plant in a location that children and pets cannot reach.

Recommended

Z. furfuracea is an upright, trunkless plant that has a tendency to spread over time. This slow-growing plant produces rigid, thick stems from a central rosette atop a large storage root. Pale green leaflets are borne opposite one another from the base of the stem to the tip and later change to olive with a rusty coating. The leaflets are stiff and cardboard-like with rounded tips. Cones are borne from fall to winter. The female cones break to reveal tightly packed, bright red seeds when ripe. Male and female cones form on separate plants.

Problems & Pests

Cardboard palms are prone to attack by scale insects, mealybugs and red spider mites.

All photos: *Z. furfuracea*

Cast Iron Plant

Aspidistra

Features: tolerates low light, neglect and dry air, upright foliage
Height: 30" (76 cm) **Spread:** 12–24" (30–61 cm)

Cast iron plant is an old favorite that is now quickly regaining popularity. Its common name is derived from its ability to tolerate a high level of neglect. It can easily withstand periods of dryness at the roots if the temperature is too high, but it is vulnerable if left too wet for long or repotted too frequently. The slow-growing *A. elatior* is the only *Apidistra* grown in cultivation and available to grow as a houseplant. It rarely flowers indoors, but in its native habitat, the flowers are pollinated by snails. The flowers often go unnoticed as a result of their location, however. Cast iron plant is ideal for those who want an easy-to-care-for plant that can thrive in low light and dry air.

Growing

Cast iron plant grows well in **bright to low light** with no direct sunlight. The **soil-based mix** should be **watered thoroughly** but infrequently, allowing the soil to almost completely dry out between waterings. It can tolerate dry air, but mist or wash the leaves periodically. It prefers average temperatures not exceeding 70° F/21°C in summer and a minimum temperature of 50° F/10° C in winter.

Tips

Cast iron plant is best displayed as a lone specimen for impact. It is sometimes difficult to find and can be expensive, but it seems to live forever. Older plants are best left in their original pots. Repot no more frequently than every 4–5 years, if necessary. Propagate by dividing when repotting in spring.

Recommended

A. elatior bears dark green leaves that emerge singly from a fleshy, creeping rootstock. Each leaf is perched on a stiff, rounded stem, on a rolled base. The leaves have prominent ribs that run from stem to tip, up to 18" (46 cm) in length. Dull purple, star-shaped flowers can occur but rarely emerge. **'Variegata'** has creamy white bands that run from stem to tip in a variety of widths.

A. elatior *is sometimes called parlor plant because it was often displayed in Victorian parlors.*

Problems & Pests

Red spider mite, scale insects and mealybugs

All photos: *A. elatior*

Century Plant

Agave

Features: succulent, spiky edged foliage, form **Height:** 4–5' (1.2–1.5 m)
Spread: 4–5' (1.2–1.5 m)

The century plant resembles the aloe plant, but aloe has soft teeth along each leaf edge whereas century plant has sharp, spiny teeth. Century plant is also often regarded as a succulent, but in fact it is a xerophyte, a type of plant able to survive in areas with little water. Although slow growing, century plant should only be grown indoors when young because a mature plant is much too large for the average home, and the spines become a hazard in a small space. Those lucky enough to have a conservatory or greenhouse will have the space for this plant to reach or exceed its mature height and spread. Flowers are sometimes produced, but rarely.

Growing

Century plant thrives in **bright light** all day, year-round. A **well-drained, loam** or **soil-based mix** amended with **coarse sand** or **perlite** should be kept **just moist** during the growing season but allowed to almost dry out

Above: *A. americana*; left & below: *A. americana* 'Marginata'

in winter. Water occasionally if the light is adequate, but allow the top two-thirds of the mix to dry out between waterings. It prefers low humidity and a normal room temperature from spring to fall, with a minimum winter temperature of 50° F/10° C.

Tips

Century plant is best grown as a magnificent specimen. In summer, place century plant outdoors in a sunny location where the spines won't hurt passersby, children or pets. Propagate by detaching 3–4" (7.6–10 cm) long offsets from the base of the plant. Leave the offsets to dry for one to two days before potting them.

If it does bloom, move it outside if it's warm enough because the flower can reach 30' (9.1 m) tall. The plant will die immediately after flowering, but without a bloom, it will last for many years in the right conditions.

Use gloves when handling the century plant to prevent injury from the spines. Some people may experience skin irritation when exposed to the sap.

Recommended

A. americana is a massive rosette of large gray-green or blue-gray,

tentacle-like leaves tipped with a needle-like spine. The sharp-edged leaves grow to 3–4' (91 cm–1.2 m) long in favorable conditions. '**Marginata**' has leaves with wide, yellow edges. '**Medio-picta**' sports leaves with a wide, central, pale yellow stripe. '**Striata**' leaves are striped yellow to white, and '**Variegata**' has leaves edged in white.

Problems & Pests

Mealybugs and root mealybugs

Removing the old, dried up leaves at the base results in a scarred, woody stem.

China Doll

Radermachera

Features: ornate, dainty foliage and form
Height: 24"–4' (61 cm–1.2 m)
Spread: 24–30" (61–76 cm)

This delicate, fern-like plant is native to southeast Asia.

T his tree-like plant thrives indoors because it tolerates the dry air prevalent in most Canadian homes. China doll was incredibly popular in the 1980s, but it eventually fell out of favor. Its increasing popularity today is welcome news to those who miss its delicate appearance. It has an Oriental look, ideal for those following Asian design trends or interested in feng shui. Its dainty exterior belies a tough plant that suits many indoor environments.

Growing

China doll grows well in **bright light** with no direct sunlight. The **soil-less** or **peat moss**–based mix should be kept **moist** at all times, or the stress from drying out can leave it vulnerable to pest infestation. Average to low humidity is best, but it benefits from an occasional misting. Normal room temperatures are best, with a minimum winter temperature of 50° F/10° C.

Tips

Pinching the tips back if it becomes too tall or straggly will maintain a more dense growth habit. Repot in spring but only if it becomes root bound. Propagate by stem cuttings or seed in the summer months.

Recommended

R. sinica (*Stereospermum sinicum*) grows into a tree-like form with a central stem supporting long, upright branches. The branches are tipped with teardrop-shaped leaflets. Each leaf is shiny and up to 2¹/₂" (6.4 cm) long. Scented, bell-shaped flowers occur but are rare. **'Variegata'** has variegated foliage.

All photos: *R. sinica*

Problems & Pests

Red spider mites, scale insects, leaf spot, mealybugs and aphids

Other common names for this plant are emerald tree and Asian bell tree, based on the flower form.

Chinese Evergreen

Aglaonema

Features: silver banded foliage, arum-like flowers and form
Height: 36" (91 cm) **Spread:** 36" (91 cm)

Chinese evergreen is grown for its variegated foliage rather than its flowers. This plant's most impressive quality is its ability to thrive in very low light, making it an ideal plant for a shady location where little else grows. Another amazing feature of this plant is its ability to remove toxins from the air. A NASA study investigating the ability of plants to remove pollutants from the air found that Chinese evergreen is one of the top ten best plants for removing formaldehyde, benzene and carbon monoxide from indoor air.

Growing

Chinese evergreen prefers **partial shade to bright light** with no direct sunlight. Higher levels of light may be necessary for varieties with near-white leaves. The **peat moss–based mix** should be kept **evenly moist**, allowing the surface to dry slightly between waterings. Younger plants require higher levels of humidity that can be generated by misting or pebble trays. Normal room temperatures are adequate, with a minimum winter temperature of 60° F/15° C.

Tips

Chinese evergreen is useful as a specimen or mixed with other plants. Use it to brighten up a space that receives little light, such as a hallway or bathroom. This plant grows best when its roots are confined, so repot only when absolutely necessary. When repotting, propagate by dividing the root ball in spring or by tip cuttings.
• All parts are poisonous, especially the small berries that emerge after the plant flowers.

Recommended

A. commutatum has spear-shaped leaves with silver markings. It grows 12" (30 cm) tall and wide and bears creamy white, arum-like flowers. 'Silver Spear' has more pronounced, mottled, silvery markings.

A. modestum grows to 24" (61 cm) with solid green leaves that are lightly narrower than those of other species. The variegated varieties are far more popular than the species, including 'Maria,' which has smaller, rounded, dark green leaves and 'Variegatum,' which displays bold cream variegated leaves.

A. pictum grows 6–18" (15–46 cm) tall and wide with dark green, velvety leaves mottled metallic gray and white.

A. pseudobracteatum grows 12–24" (30–61 cm) tall with brightly variegated leaves splashed creamy white to yellow and cream-colored stems.

A. 'Silver Queen' is a compact, low growing plant with 5–6" (13–15 cm) long leaves on short stems from soil level. The leaves are almost completely silver with green margins, edges and veins.

Problems & Pests

Mealybugs, scale insects, leaf spot, gray mold, root mealybugs and red spider mites

All photos: *Aglaonema* hybrids

Clog Plant

Nematanthus

Features: glossy, succulent foliage and orange, bubble-like flowers
Height: 6–8" (15–20 cm) **Length:** trailing stems can reach 24–36" (61–91 cm) **Spread:** 6–8" (15–20 cm) wider than the pot

Clog plant is often grown in hanging baskets because of its trailing habit. It is a stocky, dense-growing plant that bears closely spaced, tiny, succulent leaves on round, fleshy stems. Clusters of bubble-like flowers appear in between the leaves but are borne from the same location as the leaves. They're brightly colored and contrast beautifully with the dark, waxy foliage. Clog plant requires little care or maintenance.

Growing

Clog plant prefers **bright light** or **partial shade**, with some **direct sunlight** in winter. The **peat moss–based mix** should receive **moderate moisture** in summer and less in winter. Mist the leaves regularly and provide a space with average warmth and a minimum winter temperature of 50° F/10° C.

Tips

In part because of its light requirements, clog plant will need to be moved from one location to another. In winter, place the plant in a cool, brightly lit spot and cut the stems back to encourage flowering growth for the following spring. Repot every two years and propagate with stem cuttings in spring or summer.

Recommended

N. gregarius is a bushy, trailing plant with tiny, darkly colored, succulent leaves closely spaced on the stem from base to tip. Waxy, orange, swollen flowers are borne with yellow lobes. The stems can trail to 36" (91 cm) long. **'Variegatus'** has glossy green leaves with yellow centers and orange flowers.

Problems & Pests

Mealybugs

Clog plant is often confused with goldfish plant. Clog plant flowers do resemble goldfish blooms, but the two are different plants. Clog plant is Nematanthus gregarius *and goldfish plant is* Columnea x banksii.

Opposite: *N. gregarius* 'Variegatus'; this page & inset: *N. gregarius*

Coleus

Solenostemon

Features: brightly colored and patterned foliage **Height:** 6–36" (15–91 cm)
Spread: 6–36" (15–91 cm)

Many people are familiar with coleus as an outdoor bedding plant. What many don't know is that coleus also makes an ideal indoor plant. Coleus was incredibly popular in the 1970s and then almost completely disappeared, but recently it came back with a vengeance of sorts and in a vast number of new varieties. I grow it outdoors from spring through fall and bring it indoors to overwinter shortly before the first fall frost. Coleus tends to lose some of its vibrant color and can get a little straggly indoors, but if kept in a bright location and pinched back regularly, it will continue to produce brilliantly colored foliage all year.

Growing

Coleus prefers **bright light** with a **few hours of direct sunlight** daily. The **soil-based mix** should be **moist** at all times throughout the growing season and watered less during winter. Coleus requires moderate to high humidity, so mist the leaves frequently. Normal room temperatures are adequate, with a minimum winter temperature of 50° F/10° C.

Tips

Pinch out growing tips and flowers to promote bushy growth. If a plant has been overwintered, cut it back one-half to two-thirds and repot in spring to stimulate new growth from the bottom. Propagate by seeding in the spring or by stem cuttings. To obtain the same color from the original plant, use only cuttings to propagate; otherwise, the result will not look much like the parent plant. • Sap can irritate sensitive skin with repeated contact.

Recommended

S. scutellarioides (*Coleus blumei*) cultivars can grow up to 24" (61 cm), but dwarf varieties are available as well. Most have toothed, heart-shaped leaves, but there are also varieties with ruffled, fringed or lobed edges. Almost every conceivable color, pattern and mixture exist, in shades ranging from subtle to wild. Both blooming and non-blooming coleus are available. Some coleus have classic, upright forms with square stems and solid-colored leaves. '**Black Prince**' leaves are almost solid black.

'**Candidus**' is bright green with soft ivory running along the central margin and veins. '**Firebird**' has deeply lobed leaves with green edges and maroon centers. '**Glory of Luxembourg**' has soft, velvety leaves with a fiery color blend resembling flames.

Problems & Pests

Aphids, red spider mites and mealybugs

Coleus is also commonly known as flame nettle, painted nettle and poor man's croton.

All photos: *S. scutellarioides* cultivars

Croton

Codiaeum

Features: colorful, patterned foliage **Height:** 12–36" (30–91 cm)
Spread: 12–18" (30–46 cm)

*Loss of leaf color is an indication of a
lack of adequate light.*

The croton has been an integral part of indoor gardening forever it seems, and rightly so. It doesn't have to rely upon flowers for its color because this popular indoor shrub produces beautifully colored leaves in fiery shades year-round in the right conditions. Native to Malaysia, north Australia and the Pacific islands, this plant is available in a variety of forms, colors and shapes. Gardeners with any level of experience can successfully grow croton with little trouble.

Growing

Crotons require **bright light** with **some direct sunlight**. The **soil-based mix** should be kept **moderately moist** during the growing season but allowed to dry slightly between waterings in winter. Moderate to high humidity is best, with warm to normal room temperatures during the growing season and a winter minimum temperature of 60° F/16° C.

Tips

Older plants are vulnerable to leaf drop when moved from one location to another, so start with younger plants. Repot annually but only if necessary, and propagate with stem cuttings in the spring. Crotons are naturally bushy and should not require pruning. If they become too large, cut them back by one-third in early spring, and use some of the cuttings to start new plants. • All parts are poisonous if ingested, and repeated contact with sap may irritate the skin.

Recommended

C. variegatum pictum leaves are narrow to oval, lobed or forked. Some cultivars have leaves that are twisted, spiral or constricted. The pattern and coloration range from red to yellow to green and everything in between. Often a contrasting color runs along the veins, edges and margins. Fluffy, cream, ball-shaped flowers can emerge but rarely do in container-grown crotons.

Opposite & right: *C. variegatum*

'Andreanum' is compact, featuring copper-tinged green leaves and yellow-auburn veins. 'Daisy-O' has broad leaves in variegated, metallic brown-black and orange-red. 'Majesticum' has a pendulous habit with narrow, deep olive green leaves and yellow midribs maturing to crimson. 'Norma' has dark green, red and black mottled leaves with yellow veins, and 'Tortilis' has linear, twisted leaves with orange-red markings on top of green.

Problems & Pests

Red spider mites, scale insects and mealybugs

Crown of Thorns

Euphorbia

Features: spiky stems, form and tiny yellow flowers
surrounded by red or white bracts
Height: 24–36" (61–91 cm)
Spread: 12–24" (30–61 cm)

*The traditional red-bracted cultivars are
now available with white, cream, lime,
yellow, pink and bicolor bracts.*

Crown of thorns is an old favorite that remains an ideal choice for a sunny location. This plant can withstand neglect and requires little care or maintenance. This rare succulent shrub is capable of blooming year-round in adequate light, so keep crown of thorns a little more moist than you would other succulents. If allowed to dry out completely, it will go into a dormant state and lose its foliage and flowers. Crown of thorns is a unique addition to a contemporary setting.

Growing

Crown of thorns prefers **bright sunlight,** but shade it from very strong summer sun. The **soil-based mix** should include **sand** or **perlite** to improve the drainage. The mix should be kept **evenly moist** to allow the surface of the soil to dry out between waterings and water less in winter.

Tolerant of dry air, crown of thorns still benefits from the occasional misting. Normal room temperatures are suitable, with a minimum winter temperature of 55° F/13° C.

Wear gloves when handling crown of thorns.

Tips

Repot crown of thorns every two years until the plant is at least five to six years old, and then just top-dress it from that point on. Take stem cuttings in spring for propagation. Prune if necessary before new growth appears in the spring. • The sap is poisonous and should not come into contact with the eyes or mouth.

Recommended

E. milii var. *splendens* readily produces bright green, elliptical leaves on woody stems. The stems are covered in ¹/₂ –³/₄" (1.25 cm– 1.8 cm) long, sharp spines. The leaves appear only on new growth and are not replaced if they fall. Tiny, yellow flowers are produced, surrounded by red or white bracts.

All photos: *E. milii var. spendens*

Cyclamen

Cyclamen

Features: patterned foliage and colorful flowers that resemble butterflies
Height: 6–12" (15–30 cm) **Spread:** 5–10" (13–25 cm)

Without the advent of modern F1 hybrids, cyclamen simply wouldn't be seen in the average indoor garden setting. Now cyclamen is one of the most popular flowering plants available. Though most people don't keep this plant past its flowering cycle, it's fun to have even for a short time. With the right care in the best conditions, a cyclamen can last for months. Its graceful flowers resemble butterflies or upside-down flowers, and the foliage is striking. There are many jeweled colors and combinations of patterns and forms to choose from. Cyclamen is the perfect addition to any home or workplace when it's time for a short blast of color.

Growing

Cyclamen prefers **bright to moderate light** away from direct sunlight. The **soil-less mix** should be kept **moderately moist** during the growing season by using the immersion method. Medium-to-high humidity is a must, and a location with cool to cold temperatures from 50°–60° F/ 10°–15° C is ideal.

Tips

Do not pour water onto the tuber because this will cause it to rot. When flowering ceases and the foliage begins to yellow, reduce watering and stop feeding. Place the pot on its side in a cool, dry location until midsummer. In midsummer, once new growth has started, repot rested plants with the tuber only half buried. Do not increase the pot size when repotting because cyclamen flowers better if its slightly root bound. Resume normal care and maintenance. Remove faded flowers and leaves by twisting the entire stalk off at the base. To achieve the longest possible bloom, buy plants in flower or bud in early winter. If you're propagating by seed, it may take 15–18 months for standard and intermediate varieties to bloom, but miniature types can flower in approximately eight months. • The bulb and rhizomes are poisonous if ingested.

Recommended

C. persicum produces a rosette of heart-shaped leaves with green and silver markings on the upper surface and reddish purple on the lower surface. The velvety petals come in various colors, are mostly smooth or occasionally ruffled and can be fragrant. The standard series includes the

Decora Series, with pastel salmon and lavender flowers and silver-marbled leaves, and the **Sierra Series,** with over 20 intense colors. The intermediate series includes the **Laser Series,** available in 14 flower colors, which produces compact, fast-growing plants that bear up to 35 scented flowers. The miniature series includes the **Miracle Series,** with tiny scented flowers atop silvery green foliage, and the **Tiny Mites Series,** the smallest of all cyclamens, with dainty flowers. Both come in a wide range of colors.

Problems & Pests

Cyclamen mites, aphids, red spider mites and gray mold

All photos: *C. persicum*

Devil's Ivy

Epipremnum

Features: twining, glossy and variegated foliage **Height:** 6–8" (15–20 cm)
Length: trailers can grow to 8' (2.4 m) long **Spread:** 6–8' (1.8–2.4 m)

I've actually read that this plant is difficult to grow, but I beg to differ. Devil's ivy is probably one of the most common plants available to the home gardener, and justifiably so. It looks beautiful in any décor, is easy to grow and adapts to just about any indoor environment, requiring very little care and attention. In fact, it swiftly bounces back from periods of neglect. In a study done by NASA, devil's ivy was found to be one of the most effective indoor plants for removing formaldehyde molecules and cleaning the air. Versatile, attractive, functional and easy to grow—sounds like the perfect plant to me.

Growing

Devil's ivy grows best in **bright to moderate light**, yet tolerates low light levels. The **soil-less mix** should be kept **evenly moist** during the growing season and left to dry out slightly between waterings in winter. Low to moderate humidity is adequate. Mist occasionally. It prefers average warmth, with a minimum winter temperature of 50°–60° F/ 10°–15° C.

Tips

Devil's ivy bears heart-shaped leaves in myriad patterns on winding stems. If the stems are permitted to trail over the edge, keep them trimmed to a reasonable length or the center of the plant will become straggly and bare. To keep the plant bushy and dense, allow the stems to grow a little longer than the bottom of the pot. If training the stems vertically on a support, leave some of the stems long and others short for a denser plant overall. Repot if necessary in spring, and propagate by layering or stem cuttings. • All parts are poisonous if ingested and skin may become irritated with repeated contact.

Recommended

E. aureum (golden pothos, devil's ivy, hunter's robe) is a climbing or sprawling plant that can reach lengths of 6–8' (1.8–2.4 m). Thick green stems carry alternate yellow or white, variegated, shiny

foliage. Inconspicuous flowers may be produced, but rarely in pots. **'Golden Queen'** has yellow blotched leaves, and **'Marble Queen'** has boldly streaked, near-white leaves with white-marked stems. **'Neon'** is solid yellow-green and **'Tricolor'** has green leaves and stems variegated white and cream.

Problems & Pests

Aphids, mealybugs and root rot

E. aureum *is also commonly known as pothos and taro vine.*

All photos: *E. aureum*

Dracaena

Dracaena

Features: broad foliage, woody stems and overall form
Height: 24"–10' (61 cm–3 m)
Spread: 24"–4' (61 cm–1.2 m)

The *Dracaena* genus includes a wide variety of houseplants that have been wildly popular since the 19th century. Dracaenas vary in subtle ways from each other but share some physical characteristics, including strap-like foliage. Commonly mistaken for palms, these stately plants are generally easy to care for, providing a bold and attractive focal point for a foyer, hallway or living room. Tall specimens are often displayed in public spaces. They also purify the air—a NASA study found that dracaenas are some of the best plants to grow indoors to rid the air of toxic chemicals.

Growing

Generally dracaenas prefer **bright to moderate light**, shaded from direct sunlight, but they also tolerate lower light levels. The variegated varieties require bright, filtered light to maintain their foliar color. Dracaenas grow best in an **evenly moist, soil-less mix** that is allowed to dry slightly between waterings. They prefer average humidity and normal room temperatures, with a minimum winter temperature of 50°–55° F/10°–12° C. Misting occasionally is an added benefit to all except *D. goddseffiana*, which prefers dry air.

Opposite: *D. deremensis* 'Warneckii'; above: *D. marginata*
Right: *D. fragrans* 'Massangeana'

Above: *D. deremensis* 'Warneckii'
Below: *D. fragrans* 'Massangeana'

Tips

Repot no more frequently than every two years and only if necessary. Dracaenas generally have shallow root systems and grow rather slowly, so they do not need repotting as frequently as other plants. Depending on the species, propagation can be a little complicated. Air layering and stem cuttings are possible. Clean and groom the leaves often to remove dust and debris and to keep down spider mite infestations when and if they occur. Flowers may be produced but are rather insignificant. • All parts can be poisonous if ingested, especially for cats and dogs.

Leaves with brown tips and yellow edges are a sign of dry air or cold draft damage.

Recommended

D. deremensis is a slow-growing, shrub-like plant with 12–24" (30–61 cm) long, broad, strap-like leaves that emerge from a central stem or trunk. The leaves can be solid green or variegated. This plant can attain a mature height of 4–7' (1.2–2.1m). The cultivars are more common than the species. '**Bausei**' has dark green leaves with two broad, white, central bands. '**Janet Craig**' has solid green leaves and a bushy form that grows 3–5' (91 cm–1.5 m) tall and '**Janet Craig Compacta**' is a dwarf compact form. '**Warneckii**' has variegated leaves with two longitudinal white stripes parallel to the leaf edge. '**White Stripe**' and '**Yellow Stripe**' both have wide, brightly variegated bands that run along the leaf edge.

D. fragrans (corn plant, corn palm) is a shrubby tree with 24" (61 cm) long broad leaves on top of a stout trunk. Each 4" (10 cm) wide leaf forms into a crown of semi-glossy foliage perched atop a woody cane as it matures. '**Lindenii**' leaves have yellow bands down the center that almost replace the green, and '**Massangeana**' leaves have a central yellow band.

Above: *D. deremensis* 'Janet Craig Compacta'; below: *D. marginata* 'Triclor'

D. marginata (Madagascar dragon tree, red-margined dracaena) is unbranched when young but develops a clean, notched trunk and branches with age as the bottom leaves fall away. It slowly grows to 10' (3 m) and produces narrow, almost grass-like leaves 12–24" (30–61 cm) long with reddish burgundy edges. '**Colorama**' has broad red bands along the leaf edges with a yellow and green stripe down the center; '**Tricolor**' leaves feature a band of yellow separating the green and red stripes, creating an overall greenish gold effect.

Above: *D. deremensis* 'Yellow Stripe'
Below: *D. deremensis* 'Janet Craig'

Above: *D. marginata* with philodendron

D. reflexa variegata (*Pleomele reflexa*, song of India) has 6" (15 cm) long, yellow-edged green leaves on a small, branched tree or shrub reaching 3–4' (91 cm–1.2 m) in height.

D. sanderiana (Belgian evergreen, ribbon plant) has 9" (23 cm) long, white-edged green leaves on a 24–36" (61–91 cm) tall plant. Leaves grow from a central stem or trunk.

D. surculosa (*D. godseffiana*, gold dust dracaena, spotted dracaena) is more shrubby and grows to 24" (61 cm) tall. Distinctly spotted, oval leaves are produced on thin stems. **'Florida Beauty'** is heavily variegated with more cream than green. **'Kelleri'** has thicker leaves and is more spotted and marbled with ivory.

Problems & Pests
Mealybugs, scale insects, rot, red spider mites and gray mold

Most dracaenas fail as a result of overwatering, especially D. marginata *and* D. fragrans. *Water is stored in the cane-like trunks, so they're vulnerable to sitting in soil that is too moist.*

Dumb Cane
Dieffenbachia

Features: beautifully variegated foliage **Height:** 12"–6' (30 cm–1.8 m)
Spread: 12"–4' (30 cm–1.2 m)

Dumb cane has long been a favorite and regardless of trends, its popularity remains high. It's no wonder because these plants are generally easy to care for, grow moderately quickly and can brighten up even the dullest of spots. They're grown almost entirely for their striking foliage. Dumb cane flowers are insignificant, so the foliage takes center stage. Some of the more vigorous varieties can reach 6' (1.8 m) or more in six to seven years or less, so they're usually grown as large specimens rather than as compact plants. Dumb cane is available in a wide variety of patterns and sizes, enough to keep even the fussiest gardeners interested.

Growing

Dumb cane grows best in **moderate to bright light** and shaded from any direct sunlight. This plant tolerates low light; however, lack of light may adversely affect the variegation over time. It is best grown in a **peat moss–** or **soil-based mix** and should be kept **evenly moist** but allowed to dry slightly in winter. Boost humidity levels by using pebble trays and misting frequently. Dumb cane prefers normal-to-high room temperatures, with a minimum winter temperature of 60° F/16° C.

Tips

When a plant becomes too tall, cut it back by one-third. New shoots should sprout from the cut. Propagate plants when they are rootbound by taking cuttings or air layering and repotting in summer. Wear gloves when handling dumb cane, and wash your hands thoroughly afterwards. • All parts of dumb cane are poisonous if ingested. Skin may become irritated with repeated contact.

Recommended

D. x *bausei* grows 36" (91 cm) tall with 12" (30 cm) long leaves. The leaves are yellow-green with dark green margins and blotches and small white spots.

D. maculata (*D. picta*) produces a thick, cane-like stem topped with broad, lance-shaped leaves that are variegated cream and white. Occasionally, an insignificant pale green flower will emerge that looks like a rolled up leaf. This plant can reach the ceiling if allowed to grow, but try to limit its height to 6' (1.8 m).

'Camilla' grows to 12" (30 cm) with rich green, cream-edged leaves. 'Exotica' has irregularly blotched leaves in cream and pale green. 'Rudolph Roehrs' has creamy white leaves when young; as it matures, the leaves develop pale green spots with green midribs and margins.

D. seguine (dumb cane) is similar to *D. maculata* but grows more vigorously and produces longer, narrower, dark green leaves.

Problems & Pests

Aphids, rot, scale insects and red spider mites

All photos: *D. maculata* hybrids

Elephant's Ear

Alocasia

Features: large, ornate leaves on tall, skinny stems **Height:** 30" (76 cm)
Spread: 30" (76 cm)

Alocasia varieties bear spathe-like flowers, but typically not when grown in containers. The flowers are considered insignificant.

Most people are familiar with using elephant's ear in water gardens, but some may not realize that it works equally well as an indoor plant. Since elephant's ear is a little uncommon, it might be difficult to find at your local garden center except in summer. It's worth the effort, though, because its striking, enormous, arrow-shaped leaves and overall size really make a statement in any setting. Unless you have a space large enough to accommodate it, however, elephant's ear is probably better suited to a conservatory or greenhouse.

Above: *A. sanderiana*

Growing

Elephant's ear requires **partial shade** throughout the growing season and **bright light** during winter with no direct sunlight. The **soil-based mix** should be **moist** at all times but watered sparingly during the winter rest period. Allow the soil to dry out almost completely between waterings during this period. Mist occasionally. Average-to-high humidity is suitable, and warm temperatures around 70° F/21° C are best, with a minimum winter temperature of 65° F/18° C.

Tips

Divide the plants if necessary and repot to propagate. Remove dust from the leaves by gently rinsing them rather than wiping because wiping can damage the leaf surface. • All parts are very poisonous if ingested. Keep away from children and pets.

Recommended

A. x *amazonica* has dark green leaves sharply contrasted by silver veins and purple undersides. The scalloped leaves can reach 12x24" (30x61 cm) in size. 'Green Velvet' is emerald

Opposite & right: *A.* x *amazonica*

green with white veins. It can grow to double the size of *A. sanderiana*.

A. sanderiana (kris plant) has silver-green leaves with purple undersides and wavy edges. The leaves grow 12–24" (30–61 cm) long on thick, erect stems. Insignificant petal-less, arum-like flowers may emerge indoors, but rarely. 'Gandavensis' has ivory leaves with purple-red undersides and vermilion veins. 'Van Houtte' is a dwarf variety with broad leaves and gray-white midrib and veins. The species and cultivars can grow to 6' (1.8 m).

Problems & Pests

Mealybugs and red spider mites

English Ivy
Hedera

Features: twining stems clothed in decorative foliage
Height: varies with support structure **Length:** 24–36" (61–91 cm),
dependent on variety **Spread:** varies with support structure

Everyone knows English ivy in one form or another because it's easy to grow, adapts well to many conditions, grows vigorously and looks good. Available in a wide variety of sizes, colors and styles and blessed with a prolific growth habit, English ivy can be used in numerous ways indoors and outdoors, in pots or in the ground. Let it climb up or around a framework or trail over the edge of a container. Its strong, wiry stems can train themselves through the tightest of curves and around the most unusual structures with the ample support of aerial roots. With new varieties being introduced annually and new trends in decorative forms, the possibilities are endless.

Inset: *H. helix* 'Sagittifolia'; below: *H. helix* 'Ivalace'

Growing

English ivy grows best in **medium light to partial shade**. Variegated forms require some direct sunlight to maintain their color. The **soil-less mix** should be kept **consistently moist**. English ivy plants prefer cool locations if suitably acclimatized. They cannot tolerate night temperatures over 60° F/16° C, so they're more likely to thrive in an unheated room. Mist the leaves regularly in summer but only occasionally from fall to spring.

Tips

English ivy can be grown as a specimen in a hanging basket or wall planter; allow the trailers to grow beyond the bottom of the container. It can be grown as a groundcover around the base of larger floor plants or planted alongside other plants in a group or terrarium setting if kept small. Train English ivy on a variety of structures, including topiary forms, free-standing forms, hoops, obelisks and trellises. Some varieties are self-branching and require no more than an occasional pinching to remain full while others need to be pinched more often and further back on the stem. Be careful where you place certain ivies because the aerial roots cling firmly to most surfaces and can spoil walls and furnishings. Remove all solid green shoots on variegated varieties to improve and maintain leaf colorations, and propagate with cuttings. • All parts are poisonous if ingested, and skin may become irritated after contact with sap.

Recommended

H. algeriensis is a larger-leaved species with shallowly lobed leaves up to 6" (15 cm) wide. **'Gloire de Marengo'** is mottled gray-green with a white edge.

H. helix (common ivy) produces leaves that are much smaller than those of *H. algeriensis*. Numerous varieties are available with foliage in many different shapes and colors and with a variety of markings.

Common ivies can also range greatly in size. **'Glacier'** has three-lobed leaves mottled silver and cream. **'Goldheart'** has green leaves blotched with cream and yellow. **'Green Ripple'** is bushier with bright green leaves that have pale veins and a bluish cast. **'Ivalace'** (lacyleaf ivy) has five-lobed, solid green leaves with crinkled margins and edges, and **'Sagittifolia'** has an elongated central lobe, giving the leaves an arrowhead appearance.

Problems & Pests

Red spider mites are a problem but are easily eliminated by misting and an occasional bath with tepid water.

This page: *H. helix* 'Sagittifolia'

False Aralia

Schefflera

Features: serrated foliage and form
Height: 3–6'
(91 cm–1.8 m)
Spread: 12–36"
(30–91 cm)

A unique feature of false aralia is the manner in which the shape, color and size of the leaves change as they mature.

False aralia has gone through a number of name changes over the years, so don't be surprised if you find it listed under *Aralia* and *Dizygotheca*. It is also often confused with marijuana, which it resembles in form only! False aralia is a fascinating plant and a great candidate for every level of gardener. This graceful shrub produces slim, mottled stems that carry palm-like, narrow, 3" (7.6 cm) long, serrated leaves. Though the genus includes a number of species, *S. elegantissima* is the one favored as a houseplant. It demands little for its success and provides a uniquely delicate, airy display in the harshest of spaces.

Growing

False aralia requires **bright light** with no direct sunlight. The **soil-based mix** should be **thoroughly soaked** but allowed to almost dry out between waterings. Supplement humidity by using pebble trays and misting. It prefers year-round warmth with a minimum winter temperature of 60° F/16° C.

Tips

False aralia is beautiful enough to stand on its own, but it is also attractive in groupings of plants with similar requirements. It is often found growing alongside croton, cycas, devil's ivy and ti plant in its native habitat and would look equally nice in a similar indoor grouping. Prune in spring to maintain and promote bushiness, and propagate by air layering. Watch for droopy leaves, an indication of overwatering, and falling leaves, a sign that the roots were allowed to get too dry.

Recommended

S. elegantissima bears young, delicate, bronzy green foliage with serrated edges. With age the color darkens to almost green-black and the leaves becomes broader. The leaves are divided into seven to eleven finger-like leaflets that meet at a central point on erect stems. The main stems widen and become woody over time. Insignificant flowers are rarely produced. **'Castor'** has shorter, broader leaves in a dwarf or more compact form.

Problems & Pests

Aphids, mealybugs and red spider mites

Opposite: *S. elegantissima* 'Castor'
This page: *S. elegantissima*

Ferns

Adiantum, Asplenium, Davallia, Nephrolepsis, Pellaea, Platycerium

Features: ornate, lacy foliage and growth habit **Height:** 12"–5' (30 cm–1.5 m)
Spread: 12"–4' (30 cm–1.2 m)

The Boston fern will grow steadily year-round given the right conditions.

There is no end to the world of ferns. They come in just about every shape and size, leaf texture and form imaginable. Some varieties appear more fern-like than others, but all thrive in similar conditions. Some are epiphytic in their native habitat while others grow in the warm, humid environment that exists under the canopies of large trees, which is why most ferns prefer to be grown in terrariums or locations with higher humidity, including bathrooms and kitchens. With a little care and attention, you can create the perfect atmosphere for a fern to thrive.

Growing

Generally, ferns prefer **moderate to bright light** with no direct sunlight. *Asplenium* prefers shade to moderate light, and *Platycerium* ferns prefer a little direct sunlight. A well drained, **soil-based mix** should be kept **consistently moist** throughout the year. Mist often and supplement the humidity levels with pebble trays. Room temperatures not exceeding 70° F/21° C, and no cooler than 50°–60° F/10°–15° C in winter, are suitable.

Tips

Ferns are attractive in groupings, an arrangement that benefits the plants by elevating the humidity levels in their immediate vicinity. They look beautiful displayed in glass terrariums and bottle gardens, where a warm and moist environment is more consistent. Boston and button ferns are spreading ferns best grown in hanging baskets. Staghorn ferns are epiphytic and are best grown on cork bark boards or in an orchid basket lined with moss. Keep ferns

Opposite: *Davallia fejeensis*; this page, top: *Nephrolepsis exaltata* 'Fluffy Ruffles'; right: *N. exaltata* 'Bostoniensis'

Above: *Davallia fejeensis*; below: *Adiantum raddianum*

away from drafts and heat sources. Propagation can be accomplished in a variety of ways. *Asplenium bulbiferum* and *A. viviparum* can be propagated by planting plantlets or division. *Adiantum* can be divided in spring and *Nephrolepsis* can be divided or propagated by layering or by using the plantlets that develop at intervals along the rhizomes. *Pellaea* and *Platycerium* can also be divided in spring. It is sometimes difficult to repot plants in the *Asplenium* species because the roots tend to cling to the inside of the pot. Carefully running a sharp knife along the walls of the pot or gently breaking the nursery pot away from the rootball will help remove it from its container.

Platycerium should be handled with care at all times as the white, mottled coating on the fronds is easily damaged. *Adiantum* should be trimmed back if the leaflets drop. Water regularly and keep humid to encourage new growth. • All parts of *Adiantum, Asplenium, Davallia, Nephrolepsis, Pellaea* and *Platycerium* are poisonous if ingested.

Recommended

Adiantum bulbiferum (mother fern, hen and chicken fern) has more finely divided fronds. Once mature, it bears large quantities of tiny plantlets. It grows 18" (46 cm) tall.

A. capillus-vereris is a dense-growing fern with thin, feathery-looking fronds on dark stems.

A. hispidulum (Australian maiden-hair fern, rose maidenhair fern) is a coarse-looking fern whose new fronds are pinkish bronze and turn green with age. It is more upright than arching and is less delicate in appearance than other ferns.

Above: *Platycerium bifurcatum*
Below: *Nephrolepsis exaltata* 'Bostoniensis'

Basket with button fern (left), baby's tears (right)

stems that support the leaves resemble wiry, black strands of hair. **'Fragrantissima'** is similar in appearance but slightly aromatic, and **'Fritz-Luthii'** has bright green fronds.

Asplenium nidis (bird's nest fern) has broad, glossy, strap-like fronds with a central brownish margin. The fronds emerge from a central, brown, fibrous nest at the crown. Mature height and spread is 12–24" (30–61 cm).

A. viviparum (mother fern) is a slightly smaller fern with arching, lacy fronds. Similar to *A. bulbiferum*, the plantlets are borne on the fronds. It grows 24" (61 cm) tall and wide.

A. raddianum (*A. cuneatum*, delta maidenhair fern) has 8–15" (20–38 cm) long, green fronds are divided into numerous small, triangular leaflets with scalloped edges. The fronds are erect when young but arch with age. The

Davallia fejeensis (rabbit's foot fern) is a stout plant with lacy, triangular, arching fronds. It can grow 18" (46 cm) tall and 12–36" (30–91 cm) long. It's unique for the hairy rhizomes that resemble rabbit feet, which creep over the edges of the container.

Above: *Asplenium nidus*; below: *Davallia fejeensis*

Nephrolepsis biserrata (macho fern) is a new fern on the market. It bears large, wide fronds that resemble those of the Boston fern but are larger. The leaves are shiny, dark green and are less prone to drying and dropping than those of Boston fern.

N. exaltata **'Bostoniensis'** (Boston fern) produces graceful, drooping fronds up to 4' (1.2 m) long. The fronds are upright at first, then arch over slightly as they grow. Leaflets run along the central margin from the base to the tip. Brown spores line the undersides of the leaflets, and wiry runners carry young plantlets over the surface of the soil. **'Fluffy Ruffles'** has feathery leaflets in a double herringbone pattern. **'Rooseveltii'** is a large fern with wavy leaflets, and **'Smithii'** has fine lacy leaflets in a quadruple herringbone pattern. 'Whitmanii' has lacy leaflets in a triple herringbone pattern.

Pellaea rotundifolia (button fern) bears a mass of wiry stems covered in brown scales, hairs and small, round leathery leaflets. The leaflets become more oval in shape over time. The fronds are spreading in form and will trail over the edge of the pot, reaching 12" (30 cm) in length.

P. viridis (green brake fern) has black stalks and fronds that darken with age. This species grows 24" (61 cm) tall and wide with larger, more divided, feathery fronds.

Platycerium bifurcatum (staghorn fern) produces 36" (91 cm) long, fertile fronds. The grayish green, flat fronds are downy when young, resembling deer antlers. '**Majus**' is somewhat larger with erect, brighter green, fertile fronds. '**Netherlands**' has gray-green fronds that tend to be shorter and broader and radiate in all directions.

P. grande (regal elkhorn fern) has 4' (1.2 m) pale green, sterile fronds that are fan shaped with upturned edges. They are divided into long, wide, arching lobes 18"–5' (46 cm–1.5 m).

Problems & Pests
Scale insects, aphids, mealybugs, whitefly, fungal spot, root rot

Waterlogged soil will cause Pellaea *to rot and die.*

Above: *Nephrolepsis biserrata*
Center: *Nephrolepsis exaltata* 'Fluffy Ruffles'

Below: *Pellea rotundifolia*

Ficus

Ficus

Features: form, foliage **Height:** 3–6' (91 cm–1.8 m) **Spread:** 3–6' (91 cm–1.8 m)

The white latex sap of the rubber plant was once used to make rubber.

F. benjamina comprises a number of varieties. Some have single stems while others have braided stems or multiple stems. They can grow tall or remain short, the leaves can be solid green or variegated and forms can range from upright to weeping.

Ficus, or ornamental fig, is another of those indoor plants known to even the brownest of thumbs. Though all ficus plants are attractive, several of the less common varieties are especially beautiful. Ficus plants can be stately trees or low-lying creepers. Some have been popular since the early 1800s while others have fallen in and out of favor from decade to decade. There are a number of myths surrounding ficus plants that are simply not true, for instance, that if they are moved they will suffer massive leaf drop. I've always had great success with figs, and if I can grow them, so can you.

Growing

Tree-type ficus prefer **bright light** while other types prefer **partial shade**. *F. elastica* will adapt to only a few hours of early morning light, but such limited light

would prove fatal to *F. pumila*. Large-leaved and tree ficus prefer a **soil-based mix**, the top two-thirds of which should be allowed to dry slightly between waterings. Trailing types prefer a **peat moss–based mix** that requires more frequent watering. Mist the leaves of all ficus occasionally in summer, but mist year-round for the trailing types, which grow best in warm, moist air. Normal room temperatures are best for all types, with a minimum winter temperature of 50°–55° F/ 10°–13° C.

Opposite & right: *F. benjamina*

Above: *F. lyrata*

Above: *F. elastica* 'Decora'

Above: *F. elastica* 'Black Prince'

Tips

Propagate by stem cuttings in summer if the stems aren't woody. Avoid frequent repotting. Repot every two years in the spring until the plant is too large to handle.

When they are cut or injured, the leaves and stems release a resinous sap. This sap can irritate the skin and will stain fabrics and carpets.

Below: *F. elastica* 'Black Prince'

Recommended

F. benjamina (weeping fig) grows to about 6' (1.8 m) tall, with woody branches or trunk in a bush or tree form. Shiny green leaves densely cover the thin branches. The stem or trunk of tree types can either be left straight or braided for ornamental purposes. This species occasionally bears small green berries that may turn red before they fall. **'Golden Princess'** has gray-green leaves with ivory edges, and **'Starlight'** has almost white leaves with small, green blotches. **'Variegata'** is the most common type, with green leaves and creamy white edges.

F. binnendykii **'Alii'** (*F. maclellandi* 'Alii,' ladyfinger fig, Alii fig) has long, narrow, pointed, solid green leaves on woody stems. This bush grows 3–4' (91 cm–1.2 m) tall and wide.

F. deltoidea var. *diversifolia* (*F. diversifolia*, mistletoe fig) is a slow-growing bush that grows to 36" (91 cm). It bears tiny, rounded leaves with small brown spots. Pea-sized, inedible but attractive fruit is produced year-round.

F. elastica (rubber plant, rubber tree, India rubber tree) is often hard to find, but the cultivars are much more popular,

Above: *F. benjamina*

Above: *F. binnendykii*

Above: *F. benjamina* tree form

including '**Black Prince**,' which has nearly black foliage and '**Decora**,' which bears shiny, leathery leaves up to 12" (30 cm) long with pronounced midribs and red-flushed undersides. It can reach 10' (3 m) in height but usually doesn't surpass 5–6' (1.5–1.8 m) in an average home environment. It rarely flowers indoors and won't produce fruit until it reaches 30 years of age. '**Robusta**' is a sturdy plant with leaves rounder and larger than the other varieties. '**Tricolor**' produces leaves flushed with a pink hue and blotchy patches of cream, white, green and black, with a red midrib. This variety is difficult to find and a little harder to grow, but it's worth the search.

F. lyrata (fiddle leaf fig) has leaves shaped like violins. The leaves can reach 10–18" (25–46 cm) long. Rarely, it produces spherical green figs up to $1^{1}/_{4}$" (3 cm) across that are covered in tiny, fine, white dots. They're produced singly or in pairs, but only on mature trees.

F. pumila (*F. repens*, creeping fig) produces a dense carpet of foliage. The stems cling to any damp surface. The leaves are tiny, puckered and heart-shaped, and often variegated white or cream. The stems have aerial roots that will cling to a variety of surfaces, including supports for training.

Problems & Pests

Problems include red spider mites, scale insects, mealybugs and *Phomopsis* (twig dieback), a disease found in *F. benjamina*. *Phomopsis* can be prevented or controlled by not overwatering. Signs that your weeping fig has *Phomopsis* are wrinkled, loose bark and green, wilted leaves on the branch tips.

Below: *F. binnendykii* 'Alii'

Flamingo Flower

Anthurium

Features: brightly colored, waxy flowers and green, glossy foliage
Height: 12–24" (30–61 cm) **Spread:** 12–24" (30–61 cm)

Flamingo flower is as exotic as it sounds. It's no surprise that this plant is native to wet mountain forests in tropical and subtropical parts of North and South America. The bright red, glossy flowers are very unusual and appear

almost artificial. With the right care, and in the best location, flamingo flower will provide color for months. The flowers last and last—great for a dramatic effect. This genus is reasonably tolerant of ordinary room conditions, but increasing the humidity is beneficial and lends to its longevity.

Growing

Flamingo flower prefers **bright, indirect sunlight** in winter with some shade in summer. The **peat moss–based mix**, with added sphagnum moss, should be **well drained** but **consistently moist** at all times. Mist the leaves frequently to increase the air humidity. Avoid spraying the flowers. It requires average warmth, with a minimum winter temperature of 60° F/16° C.

Tips

Remove any dust from the leaves with a gentle rinse rather than wiping, which can cause damage to the leaf surface. The flowers may need staking for support, or gently wrap fine, plastic-covered wire around the stems. Cover any aerial roots that may emerge from the stem with sphagnum moss or insert them into the potting mix. Repot every two years in spring and propagate by division, stem cuttings or seed. • If ingested, all parts may cause nausea, and contact with the sap may irritate skin.

Recommended

A. andraeanum (flamingo lily, oilcloth flower) can grow 12" (30 cm) tall and wide in an upright form. The heart-shaped leaves arch back and can grow to 12" (30 cm) long. Bright red, glossy spathes emerge on tall, wiry stems. A central, yellow spadix is produced from the stem and the flower's edge.

A. crystallinum (crystal Anthurium, strap flower) grows upright with large, heart-shaped leaves. The leaves emerge bronzy pink but mature to a deep, olive green with pale green veins and margins. The leaves can grow to 12" (30 cm) or more in length and extend away from the center. The plants can reach 24" (61 cm) tall and wide. Flowers may emerge but are insignificant.

Opposite & right: *A. scherzerianum*

Above: *A. crystallinum*

A. scherzerianum (flamingo flower, pigtail plant) produces 6–8" (15–20 cm) long, oval-shaped leaves that stand upright on wiry stems. It can reach 24" (61 cm) tall and wide. Bright red flowers are borne intermittently throughout the year with twisted, orangy red spadices. **'Rothschildianum'** has red flowers with white spots and yellow spadices, and **'Wardii'** has red stems and large, dark red flowers with long, red spadices.

Problems & Pests

Mealybugs, red spider mites, aphids and leaf spot fungus

Flowering Maple

Abutilon

Features: pendent, pastel flowers and maple-like foliage
Height: 4–5' (1.2–1.5 m) **Spread:** 24–36" (30–91 cm)

Flowering maple is a vigorous shrub that may need a little room to spread. It's not difficult to grow, despite its exotic appearance. It can be trained into a standard or topiary form with a little pruning or left alone as a specimen. It bears pendent blooms on slender stalks between early summer and fall. I put my flowering maple outside from spring to fall, when there's no risk of frost. Soon after bringing it in for winter, it usually sends out a flush of blooms for a month or so. While most other plants go dormant in winter, my flowering maple continues to grow taller and wider with every month as spring approaches. It requires so little and gives so much back.

Growing

Flowering maple requires **bright light** with **direct sunlight**. The **soil-less mix** should be **thoroughly soaked** and allowed to almost completely dry out between waterings. It tolerates moderate humidity but doesn't mind an occasional misting. Normal to cool room temperatures are best, with a minimum winter temperature of 60° F/16° C.

Tips

With its vigorous growth habit, flowering maple can become top heavy, so plant it in a container such as one made from ceramic or clay. Prune it back by one-third in spring to prevent it from growing out of control and to maintain bushiness. When bringing it inside for winter, cut it back by half and gently rinse the leaves and stems of dirt and pests. Leave it in quarantine for a month or so until you can ensure that it is clean. Propagate the stem cuttings when pruning or sow new plants from seed.

Recommended

A. x *hybridum* (flowering maple) is a bushy shrub. It bears downy, maple-like leaves on woody branches. The single flowers are pendulous and bell-shaped. Many varieties are available in colors including peach, white, cream, yellow, orange, red and pink. Variegated cultivars are also available. Many of the variegated varieties bloom as abundantly as the solid green ones, but some with stronger variegations bloom weakly and make better foliage plants. 'Boule de Neige' has white flowers, 'Canary Bird' bears yellow flowers and 'Cannington Red' has golden yellow leaves and striking red blooms. 'Fireball' has red flowers, and 'Kentish Belle' bears vibrant orange

flowers. 'Pink Lady' has bright pink flowers with deeper pink veins and 'Souvenir de Bonn' has medium pink flowers.

A. megapotamicum (weeping Chinese lantern) is a trailing plant suitable for hanging baskets or training up a vertical support. It produces arrow-shaped 3" (7.6 cm) long leaves. Lantern-like flowers hang down from the wiry stems. 'Variegatum' has yellow-splashed leaves.

A. pictum (*A. striatum*, spotted flowering maple) may be the best known variety. This vigorous shrub can reach 5' (1.5 m) or more and bears yellow or yellow-orange flowers with deep crimson veins. 'Gold Dust' produces orange flowers and light green leaves heavily mottled with gold. 'Thompsonii' is upright but compact with mottled yellow foliage and salmon-flushed orange flowers.

Problems & Pests

Mealybugs, aphids, whiteflies and cylamen mites can all cause damage.

All photos: *A* x *hybridum* cultivars

Gardenia

Gardenia

Features: crisp, white, fragrant flowers and dark green foliage
Height: 12–24" (30–61 cm) typically; can be trained into a standard and allowed to grow taller for effect
Spread: 12–24" (30–61 cm)

Fumes from natural gas appliances will cause gardenias to wilt and die.

The frangrant scent of gardenia reminds me of flowery tropical destinations. The waxy flowers and super glossy foliage are so pure and perfect, the plant seems artificial. Gardenias are native to east Asia but are commonly found cultivated in such tropical places as Hawaii. The scent is often used in perfumes or scented bath or cleaning products, and with good reason—it's powerful and unforgettable. Several varieties of gardenia are available from the 250 species within the genus, but only a few are suited to indoor cultivation.

Growing

Gardenias prefer **bright light** but should be kept out of direct midday sunlight in summer. The **soilless, humus-rich mix** should be **moist** at all times. Reduce watering slightly in winter. Mist the leaves frequently to increase the humidity, but do not mist the flowers. Gardenias require average warmth, with a minimum winter temperature of 60° F/16° C.

Tips

Prune gardenias in late winter to maintain a good shape. While pruning, take stem cuttings for propagating and repot every two to three years in spring. Watch for these warning signs—yellowing leaves may indicate too much shade, the flowers may drop if the air is too dry, and the foliage may become pale and yellow if the water has a high lime content. If you suspect your water has a high lime content, use only filtered water and apply chelated iron every two weeks for a couple of months twice annually.

All photos: *G. augusta*

Recommended

G. augusta (*G. jasminoides*, gardenia, jasmine, cape jessamine) features semidouble or double blooms with waxy white petals. The flowers are borne on the tips of stems that become woody over time. The leaves are 4" (10 cm) long, deep, dark green and glossy. The intensely fragrant flowers bloom from summer to fall, are 3" (7.6 cm) across and resemble open rose blossoms.

Problems & Pests

Whitefly, mealybug, scale insects and red spider mites can all cause damage. Stem canker is also a problem, caused by the fungus *Phomopsis gardeniae*.

Grape Ivy
Cissus

Features: beautiful foliage and a trailing but bushy form
Height: 5–10' (1.5–3 m) **Length:** trailers can reach 10' (3m)
Spread: depends on width of support structure

Pinch shoot tips back to keep plants more compact and under control. If they become bare at the base, cut them back by one-third in spring.

Grape ivy has been a favorite indoor plant for decades. Generally a vigorous, scrambling kind of plant, grape ivy can cover large areas with its foliage in a short period of time. It is suitable for a wide range of conditions and is well liked because it's adaptable and tolerates low light levels and dry air. The flowers are inconspicuous, but the foliage and form come together to create a lush, attractive specimen.

Growing

Grape ivy grows in **moderate light** with no exposure to direct sunlight. It can tolerate light shade and will adapt to a variety of light conditions. Keep the **soil-** or **peat based–mix evenly moist** throughout the growing season, but allow it to dry out slightly between waterings in winter. Mist occasionally to prevent the leaf tips from browning. Average humidity is best in cool conditions, with a minimum winter temperature of 50° F/10° C in winter.

Tips

Grape ivy is often sold in hanging baskets, but it can also be trained on a vertical support for a different look. When training this plant, make sure the supports are well anchored to provide a stable base for the weighty stems and foliage. Propagate by taking tip cuttings in spring and early summer. • The berries are poisonous if ingested.

Recommended

C. antarctica (kangaroo vine) is a vigorous, woody climber that can grow to 10' (3 m) or more. The heart-shaped leaves have toothed edges, a dark and glossy surface and pale undersides. Forked tendrils, which the plant uses to climb, are located on the opposite side of the stem from some leaves. Insignificant flowers are borne in small clusters. '**Minima**' is a dwarf, slow-growing form with spreading horizontal branches.

C. rhombifolia (grape ivy, oak leaf ivy) can reach 10' (3 m) in height. Three coarsely toothed leaflets are produced on wiry stems. New growth is covered in fine hairs, which makes leaves appear silvery when young, but leaves become a dark, glossy green with age. '**Ellen Danica**,' also known as mermaid vine, has dark green, lobed leaflets. '**Mandaiana**' bears erect stems that spread when the plant matures. The leaves are tough but smooth, and tendrils appear only as the plant reaches maturity.

Problems & Pests

Aphids and red spider mites

Opposite & above: *C. rhombifolia*
Right: *C. rhombifolia* 'Ellen Danica'

Jade Plant

Crassula

Features: succulent foliage, branched form and tiny flowers
Height: 3–6' (91 cm–1.8) **Spread:** 24–36" (61–91 cm)

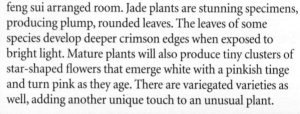

Jade plants are succulents that grow into a stocky tree form. They have an Oriental look, making them especially suitable for any Asian-themed décor or feng sui arranged room. Jade plants are stunning specimens, producing plump, rounded leaves. The leaves of some species develop deeper crimson edges when exposed to bright light. Mature plants will also produce tiny clusters of star-shaped flowers that emerge white with a pinkish tinge and turn pink as they age. There are variegated varieties as well, adding another unique touch to an unusual plant.

Growing

Jade plants prefer **bright light**. The **soil-less** or **cactus mix** should be **thoroughly drenched** and **let to dry out** almost completely before watering again. They prefer average humidity and tolerate dry air. Normal to cool temperatures are best, with a minimum winter temperature of 45°–50° F/7°–10° C.

Above: *C. ovata*

Tips

When pruning, dust the wounds with sulfur or ash to stop the flow of sap, but prune only if necessary. Mist the leaves occasionally to remove dust and debris. To prevent the plant from becoming straggly, provide enough light, and move it to a cooler location if the leaves begin to drop. Propagate by leaf and tip cuttings in spring.

Recommended

C. arborescens (jade plant, silver jade plant) can reach 4–6' (1.2–1.8 m) heights if conditions are suitable. It grows into a tree form from branched, fleshy but firm stems that are covered in brown bark. The fleshy leaves are 1–2" (2.5–5.1 cm) wide, almost round and gray-green rimmed with red. 'Variegata' is a slower growing variety with creamy white and yellowish leaf markings.

C. ovata (*C. portulacea*, jade tree) grows 3–6' (91 cm–1.8 m) tall with branched stems covered in peeling bark and shiny green, thick leaves with either red or pale green margins. White, starry flowers, tinged pink, may emerge in

Center: *C. ovata* 'Tricolor'

spring on mature plants. 'Crosby's Compact' has a dwarf habit with rounded, bronze-purple leaves. 'Dwarf Green' has dark green leaves tipped with burgundy, and 'Sunset' has glossy, green leaves striped yellow and edged in red. 'Tricolor' is a variegated variety.

Problems & Pests

Gray mold, mealybugs, weevil grubs, rot

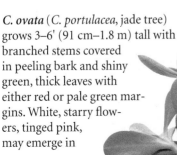

Opposite & right: *C. ovata*

Japanese Sago Palm
Cycas

Features: comb-like foliage and brown base **Height:** 24"–6' (61 cm–1.8 m)
Spread: 24"–4' (61 cm–1.2 m)

This plant is native to Japan, where it grows under tree canopies. Plants may live for decades; 50–60-year-old specimens aren't uncommon.

Japanese sago palm is an example of a common name being a little deceiving. This exotic-looking plant isn't a palm at all but a cycad, a primitive plant that dates back millions of years before even dinosaurs roamed the earth. A Japanese sago palm is a living piece of natural history—and certainly easier to care for than your average dinosaur! Easy to find, this plant can be pricey because of its incredibly slow growth habit—it produces only one new set of leaves annually and can generate large red seeds, but only when both male and female are present, and supplemented by hand pollination.

Growing

Japanese sago palm prefers **bright, indirect sunlight**. Grow in equal parts of a **soil-based medium, peat moss** and **coarse sand** or **perlite**. Allow the soil to dry slightly between thorough waterings. Water less in winter, especially if the temperatures are cooler. Normal room temperature is best, with a minimum winter temperature of 50° F/10° C.

Tips

A Japanese sago palm has a unique appearance, starting with its brown, pineapple-shaped base or stem. From this stem, feathery fronds similar to those of ferns emerge. These tender young leaves are easily damaged, so take care when handling them. Once the fronds have hardened off, they become rigid with sharp tips. Watch for brown spots or patches on the leaves, a sign of over-watering, and yellowing leaves, evidence of underwatering. If necessary, repot every two to three years in spring or fall. Propagation isn't recommended.

Recommended

C. revoluta has a brownish, pineapple-shaped stem or base. Loose rosettes or feathery fronds emerge from this stem and grow to be about 36" (91 cm)

All photos: *C. revoluta*

long. Each frond consists of a stiff, central margin lined with closely packed and sharply pointed, needle-like leaflets. The leaflet pattern resembles a comb. New inner fronds grow vertically but arch over time.

Problems & Pests

Scale insects, mealybugs and red spider mites

Jasmine
Jasminum

Features: fragrant flowers borne on twining stems **Height:** 10' (3 m)
Length: trailers reach 5–10' (1.5–3 m) **Spread:** depends on support structure

Jasmine is a vigorously growing vine with intensely scented blossoms. It is part of a genus consisting of approximately 200 species. Because of jasmine's vigorous growth habit, some people prefer to grow it in a space where it can grow freely without constraints and in the conditions it requires to thrive. Ideally, the best place to grow jasmine is in a conservatory, greenhouse, atrium or sunroom, but you can get away with a bright and sunny location in a more standard indoor environment. It's very easy to train jasmine onto any kind of support structure as long as its size is controlled with pruning. The pink jasmine is considered the easiest to grow.

Growing

Jasmine prefers **moderate to bright light** with **some direct sunlight**. The **soil-based mix** should be kept **moist** during the growing season. Allow the surface of the mix to dry out slightly between waterings in winter, but mist the foliage regularly. Jasmine prefers normal to cool room temperatures, with a minimum winter temperature of 50°–60° F/10°–18° C.

Tips

Grow jasmine in a large container with a suitable support. Prune it back once or twice annually to contain its size and prevent it from becoming straggly. Jasmine can be grown outdoors in summer in a bright location. It can be propagated by cuttings and repotted in the spring. Black leaves are an indication of a location that is too cool. Remove the affected leaves, and move the plant to a warmer location. • All parts are poisonous if ingested.

Recommended

J. mesnyi (*J. primulinum*, primrose jasmine) produces non-twining stems clothed in leaves made up of three leaflets each. The bright yellow, unscented flowers are semi-double in form, 1–1 ¹/₂" (2.5–3.8 cm) across with six or more petals. Cultivars are available with double flowers that emerge where the leaf meets the stem.

J. officinale (white jasmine) is a climber with divided leaves and loose sprays of scented, white flowers. The flowers have long, tubular throats that open into a five-petalled, star-shaped 'face.' **'Affine'** blooms more

Above: *J. polyanthum* with cyclamen

profusely than the species and has larger flowers with pink exteriors.

J. polyanthum (pink jasmine, Chinese jasmine) is similar to *J. officinale* but bears pink buds that open into white, starry, fragrant flowers. The twining stems are covered in five to seven leaflets per leaf.

Basic rules to follow when growing jasmine: choose a cool location in winter; place it outdoors in summer; and provide plenty of light and support.

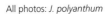
All photos: *J. polyanthum*

Kalanchoe

Kalanchoe

Features: colorful flowers, glossy or fuzzy foliage
Height: 6–18" (15–46 cm)
Spread: 10–30" (25–76 cm)

*Once sold as a Christmas flowering plant,
flaming Katy is available year-round. It is still
sold by the name Christmas kalanchoe.*

Of all the kalanchoe species and cultivars available, the most popular is flaming Katy or *K. blossfeldiana*. The *Kalanchoe* genus includes an extremely varied group of plants, all of which are succulent to some degree. There are fuzzy ones and waxy ones, species that cascade and others that grow vertically, species grown for foliage and others grown strictly for flowers. All varieties are easy to grow, add interest to any interior setting and require little care or attention. Kalanchoe is also one of the few indoor plants that offers color at an otherwise dreary time of the year.

Kalanchoes are tolerant of dry air, so they make great plants for centrally heated homes.

All photos: *K. blossfeldiana*

Growing

Kalanchoe requires **bright light** including **some direct sunlight,** but avoid direct summer sun through glass during the hottest part of the day. The **soil-based mix** with **added sand** or **perlite** should be **watered thoroughly,** but allow the surface to dry between waterings. Mist only the kalanchoe varieties with smooth leaves occasionally. They generally prefer average warmth, with a minimum winter temperature of 50° F/10° C.

Above: *K. blossfeldiana*

Above: *K. beharensis*

Tips

When selecting a *K. blossfeldiana* specimen, choose one with bright and fresh looking stems carrying plenty of unopened buds. Kalanchoe is easily propagated by stem cuttings. Plant

Below: *K. beharensis*

offsets in spring or summer. Once *K. blossfeldiana* has finished blooming, trim one quarter of the stems back and place in a shady location. Keep the potting mix nearly dry for approximately a month, then place it in a well-lit spot and water normally. Repot annually in spring after its rest period.

Recommended

K. beharensis (velvet leaf) has large, grayish green fleshy leaves with burgundy markings and edges. The fuzzy leaves emerge from a central stem.

K. blossfeldiana (flaming Katy) is a bushy, upright growing plant featuring rounded, fleshy leaves with scalloped edges. Flowers come in yellow, peach, red, white and pink and are borne in large clusters on 12–18" (30–46 cm) tall plants. Miniature varieties are available as well. '**Calypso**' has dark leaves and deep pink flowers.

K. manginii has fleshy, oval leaves and bears large, pendent, bell-shaped flowers in fiery and peachy shades. '**Tessa**' has reddish, wiry stems and loose panicles of drooping salmon or pink flowers with green tips. '**Wendy**' has deep purple, drooping flowers with peach edges.

K. marmorata (pen wiper) produces blue-green, rounded, fleshy leaves with purple-brown markings and scalloped edges. White, starry-shaped flowers with long, narrow throats emerge from the center.

K. pumila is a low-growing, branching plant covered in oval leaves with toothed edges. A white, waxy coating makes the leaves appear blue-green in color. Tiny, pale purple flowers are borne in clusters. This species is best grown in a hanging basket.

K. tomentosa (panda plant, pussy ears) grows to 18" (46 cm) and bears gray-green leaves that form a rosette.

Above: *K. marmorata*; below: *K. tomentosa*

The leaves are covered in a silvery 'fur,' and the tips and margins are marked with brown.

Problems & Pests
Mealybugs

Leaf Flower

Breynia

Features: colorful variegated foliage and shrubby form **Height:** 4' (1.2 m)
Spread: 24–36" (61–91 cm)

Leaf flower is the only member of the genus *Breynia* that is commonly grown as an indoor plant. Introduced years ago as an indoor plant, leaf flower never really caught on. It's now more popular but not yet widely available. Still, it's worth the search. Leaf flower is a shrubby, colorful plant with variegated leaves and tiny green flowers that brightens up the darkest of spaces. It does require an extremely moist environment to grow well, which can be created by misting, terrariums, groupings and pebble trays. Its uniqueness will add a different flavor to the mix.

Growing

Leaf flower prefers **bright, filtered light** with no direct sunlight. The **soil-based mix** should be kept **moist** at all times. It requires plenty of humidity year-round, so mist frequently and place the pot on a pebble tray. Average room temperatures are fine, with a minimum winter temperature of 60° F/16° C.

Tips

Prune it back by one-third each spring to maintain its size, and use the cuttings for propagation. Repot every second spring.

Recommended

B. nivosa (B. disticha) has slender, zigzagging pink stems densely clothed in green leaves with white marbling.

Leaf flower, also known as snow bush, is native to tropical parts of Asia, the South Pacific and Australia.

Opposite & right: 'Rosea-Picta'
Above: *B. nivosa*

'**Rosea-Picta**' is more popular than the species. It bears green foliage marked with white and pink, which is often mistaken for flowers. '**Atropurpurea**' has dark purple leaves.

Problems & Pests

Red spider mites, whiteflies and aphids

Lipstick Plant

Aeschynanthus

Features: tubular, lipstick-like flowers and succulent oval foliage
Height: 24" (61 cm) **Spread:** 18" (46 cm)

The lipstick plant is an epiphytic plant that grows on trees in its native habitat and closely resembles its relative, the goldfish plant. It is often sold in hanging baskets because of its pendulous, sprawling habit. Also known as basket vine, this blooming trailer has simple needs and requires a rest period during the winter months. It blooms profusely for lengthy periods, bearing flowers that resemble tubes of lipstick about every second year. It is ideal for a home or work environment.

Growing

Lipstick plant prefers **bright light** with up to **two to three hours of direct sunlight** in winter and filtered sunlight in summer. A mixture of **equal parts** of **coarse peat, perlite** and **leaf mold** should be **watered thoroughly** and allowed to dry slightly between waterings. Water more frequently when in flower and less during its winter rest period. High humidity is a must with normal room temperatures, and a minimum winter temperature of 55° F/12° C.

Tips

If placed in a humid location, lipstick plant will not have a rest period, which means consistent, year-round watering and attention will become necessary. Repot the plant when it becomes root-bound and propagate by cuttings or layering. Once flowering is complete, cut the stems back if they are straggly and place it in a bright location in winter.

Recommended

A. lobbianus produces pale green leaves with a purplish edge and a waxy surface. Bright, tubular flowers emerge from a narrow, brownish purple sheath.

A. mamoratus (zebra basket vine) is grown mostly for its foliage. It bears shiny, mottled, dark green leaves with red-flushed undersides and greenish yellow, somewhat insignificant flowers.

A. speciosus (basket plant) has yellow-orange flowers with red markings. The stems grow to 24" (61 cm) long and are clothed in 3" (7.6 cm) long, erect flowers with yellow bases that darken to red mouths.

Problems & Pests

Aphids

Lipstick plant is native to tropical rain forests, where it thrives in the high humidity.

Opposite & right: *A. lobbianus*

Lucky Bean

Castanospermum

Features: foliage and bean-like stem base **Height:** 3'–4' (91 cm–1.2 m)
Spread: 24–36" (61–91 cm)

Lucky bean plant, or black bean tree, is often found for sale prior to St. Patrick's Day. It is said that the base-like beans from which the stems emerge are the same lucky beans that Jack planted, which later became the beanstalk he climbed to meet the giant. While I don't know about that, I can say for certain that lucky bean is a very popular landscaping tree in Australia and is quickly gaining popularity in North America as an indoor plant. The common name is derived from the large seed pod the plant produces after flowering. Lucky bean is a vigorous, beautiful foliage plant and simply a curiosity that's bound to drum up a little conversation at your next party.

Growing

Lucky bean prefers a **bright** location with some **direct sunlight**, but will also tolerate light shade. The **well-drained, soil-based mix** should be kept **evenly moist** but allowed to dry slightly between waterings. Mist occasionally and provide a space with moderate temperatures and a minimum winter temperature of 50° F/10° C. Lucky bean can tolerate temperatures as low as 14° F/-10° C.

The 'bean' eventually shrivels and comes away from the base of the stems.

Tips

Soon after bringing lucky bean home, you'll find that it begins to produce an abundance of new growth. New foliage will be twice as large as existing leaves and may overwhelm the plant. Remove the newer foliage to maintain a bushier form. Lucky bean is often maintained as a bonsai or standard when only one stem is present, but there can be one to three stems per pot. This plant benefits from short periods in a sheltered outdoor location in summer.
• Seeds are toxic if ingested.

will emerge from a rounded, split, succulent 'bean', formerly the seed, at soil level. Branches form from this stem, carrying leaves composed of five to ten leaflets. Once the flowers are spent, if they're produced at all, seedpods begin to form, enclosing large seeds.

Problems & Pests
Red spider mites

Recommended

C. australe is a vigorous evergreen tree, capable of growing to ceiling height but better kept to a smaller size with pruning and training. Colorful, tightly packed clusters of orange flowers can be produced, but rarely are in pots. A central stem

Lucky bean is tolerant of low humidity and neglect and won't drop its leaves when stressed.

All photos: *C. australe*

Ming Aralia

Polyscias

Features: parsley-like foliage and graceful form
Height: 6–8' (1.8–2.4 m)
Spread: 24–36" (61–91 cm)

Ming aralias are ideal for Asian-themed rooms and for training into bonsai.

I rescued an ailing Ming aralia from a group of plants that I maintained in an office over 10 years ago. It was only 18" (46 cm) tall and in serious trouble. It is now 7' (2.1 m) tall, lush and full and a conversation piece. A Ming aralia has a look matched by few other houseplants. It can be a little hard to find at times and somewhat expensive, but I highly recommend this beauty to anyone with a taste for something different.

Growing
A Ming aralia requires **bright light** and at least **a half day of direct sunlight**. It can also adapt to locations with light shade. Keep the **soil-based mix moderately moist** but let it dry slightly between waterings, especially in winter. Warm to average temperatures are best, with minimum winter temperatures of 55°–60° F/13°–16° C. It prefers higher humidity, so frequent misting is beneficial.

Tips
As a Ming aralia grows taller, the green stems may need support until they become woody. Prune it back in spring by one-third to maintain bushiness if necessary. Propagate by stem cuttings in spring. • All parts are poisonous if ingested. Skin may be irritated by repeated contact with foliage.

Recommended
P. x *crispata* (chicken gizzard) has crinkly, overlapping foliage in a compact form.

P. fruticosa (ming aralia) is a shrub or small tree with finely cut, parsley-like foliage on twisted, branching stems from a main trunk or group of trunks. The leaves are divided into irregular and saw-edged leaflets. Small, greenish, insignificant flowers may be produced but rarely in pots.

P. x *marginata* (dinner plate aralia) is a shrub featuring large, rounded green leaves with white margins and edges.

P. scutellaria is a shrub or small, narrow tree that grows 6–8' (1.8–2.4 m) tall. It produces rounded leaves on long, wiry stems that emerge from woody branches. The leaves can have wavy or smooth edges. '**Balfourii**' (Balfour aralia) has

Above: *P. scutellaria* 'Balfourii'

smaller leaves speckled gray-green that also often have white, toothed edges. '**Pennockii**' bears 3–4" (7.6–10 cm) oval leaves mottled white and yellow-green on a 36" (91 cm) tall, dwarf shrub. Inconspicuous flowers may be produced, but not often.

Problems & Pests
Scale insects and red spider mites

Opposite & right: *P. fructicosa*

Monkey Plant

Ruellia

Features: purple foliage and flowers **Height:** 18–24" (46–61 cm)
Spread: 18–24" (46–61 cm)

I discovered monkey plant earlier this year and have grown quite fond of this little beauty. The leaves have a velvety surface and are deep green tinged purple with prominent silvery veins. Often you'll find this plant in bloom in your local garden center, showing off its trumpet-shaped, bright pinky purple flowers. Also known as the trailing velvet plant, monkey plant is usually sold in hanging baskets. I prefer to pinch out the tips from time to time to prevent the stems from cascading over the pot's edge, however. It doesn't seem to mind being forced to be a compact, almost shrubby specimen, and it blooms at least twice a year.

Growing

Monkey plant prefers to grow in **bright, indirect sunlight**. It requires a **soil-based mix**, with added **sand** for drainage. The mix should be kept **moist** throughout the flowering cycle but allowed to dry slightly between waterings. After it flowers, water just enough to keep it from drying out for one to two months and allow it to rest. Mist often to maintain higher humidity levels or place pot on a pebble tray. Average warmth is best, with a minimum winter temperature of 55° F/12° C.

Tips

Because of its trailing habit, monkey plant is often sold in hanging baskets, a presentation that complements the plant very well. It is beautiful in a decorative pot displayed on a plant stand or in a space where the stems can trail freely. When trained to remain compact, monkey plant works well grouped with silvery, light-colored or variegated plants for contrast. Monkey plants should be propagated by tip cuttings or division and repotted in spring, but only if rootbound.

Monkey plants prefer a location that is warm and humid.

Recommended

R. makoyana produces tender stems that carry deep purple–tinged, velvety green leaves with silvery veins. The color will fade and revert back to solid green in shaded locations. The bright, pink-purple flowers are approximately 2" (5.1 cm) long and resemble tiny, flared trumpets.

Problems & Pests

Aphids

All photos: *R. makoyana*

174

Norfolk Island Pine

Araucaria

Features: needle-covered, horizontal branches and form
Height: 36"–6' (91 cm–1.8 m) **Spread:** 4–5' (1.2–1.5 m)

*Norfolk Island
pine was discovered
on Norfolk Island
in the South Pacific
by Sir Joseph Banks
in 1793.*

N orfolk Island pine is statuesque in form, height and spread and a welcome departure from the norm. This long-lived plant can reach 200' (61 m) in its native habitat but takes many decades to grow that tall. It closely resembles outdoor evergreen pines, which require a large space to mature over time. Norfolk Island pine is one of the few conifers that can be used in an interior setting because it's easy to grow and maintain, it's slow to reach its mature height and it suits a variety of environments. When tiny and young, this plant can be grown in terrariums. Often it's grown as a bold specimen plant in a foyer, large room or hallway.

Growing
Norfolk Island pine prefers **bright light** with **some direct sunlight**. The **soil-based mix** should be kept **moist** from spring to fall, but watered less in winter. Mist the foliage occasionally, especially during warm and dry periods. Cool to average room temperatures are best, with minimum winter temperatures of 50° F/10° C.

Tips
Hot, dry air is detrimental to Norfolk Island pine. Keep it away from heat registers and radiators or leaf drop and loss of lower branches will occur. Allow it to become rootbound to restrict its growth. Repot only if necessary and not more than every three to four years. It may enjoy periods outdoors during summer in a location with bright but filtered light. Pruning isn't advisable, but remove bare lower branches to encourage bushier growth if it becomes straggly. Propagation isn't recommended.

Recommended
A. heterophylla (*A. excelsa*) is a slow-growing evergreen tree with a central stem or trunk and widely spaced, thin, stiff branches that are covered in soft needles. The needles become more rigid and prickly with age. Flowers and cones are rarely produced in pots.

Problems & Pests
Aphids and mealybugs

All photos: *A. heterophylla*

Orchids

Cattleya, Cymbidium, Dendrobiums, Oncidiums, Phalaenopsis

Features: ornate, colorful and exotic flowers perched above low-growing foliage **Height:** 24–36" (61–91 cm) **Spread:** 12–18" (30–46 cm)

Is there anything more beautiful than an orchid? I agree with my mother, who adores orchids, and believes that they are possibly the most exotic and beautiful of any flower. Orchids are available in many patterns and colors, touching every spectrum of the rainbow. The flowers are often alternately produced on tall, wiry stems far above the foliage. Even the foliage varies, from the strap-like leaves of the *Cymbidium* to the tongue-like leaves of the *Phalaenopsis*. Mother Nature has also brilliantly endowed orchids with the perfect combination of form, shape and color to attract the insects necessary for their pollination. Orchids are not only stunning to look at, they are fascinating plants.

Growing

Epiphytic orchids require **bright light** shaded from direct sunlight. The **orchid mix** should be **well-drained** and **moistened thoroughly**, but the top half inch should be allowed to dry between waterings. Water less during cool periods. Supplement humidity levels with pebble trays. A well-ventilated location is a must. Optimum temperatures for individual types vary, but the general rule is a day temperature of about 70° F/21° C in summer and 60° F/16° C in winter.

Terrestrial orchids require **medium light** with little to no direct sunlight. The **orchid mix** should be **well-drained** and kept **moderately moist** during the active growth cycle, but the top half inch should be allowed to dry between waterings. Water less for one to two months immediately after flowering. Mist frequently when temperatures exceed 65°–70° F/18°–21° C, and supplement humidity levels with pebble trays.

Opposite: *Cymbidium* hybrids; this page: *Phalaenopsis* hybrids

Above: *Oncidium* hybrid

Tips

Orchids are not tolerant of hot and stuffy conditions, so provide a well-ventilated location for all types. Avoid placing them in cold drafts, but do put them outside on warm summer days. They prefer being rootbound, so don't worry if a few roots escape the confines of the pot. Repot every two years when the growth begins to suffer, and divide when necessary as a means of propagation. When dividing, leave at least three shoots on each division. Stake newly potted plants, and support flower stems as they emerge to prevent them from damage.

Recommended

Cattleya orchids (corsage orchids) are sympodial epiphytes, meaning they have many stems arising from a hori-

zontal rhizome. They bear beautiful, waxy flowers 4–6" (10–15 cm) across. The flowers are borne singly or in small groups in colors including pink, white and purple with a bright center. Often the bottom petal-like lip is ruffled and a deeper, darker shade than the other five petal-like parts.

Cymbidium hybrids are regarded as beginner's orchids because they are easy to grow. On average, they reach heights of 24–36" (61–91 cm). The hybrids include sympodial, epiphytic and semi-terrestrial types. They bear upright spikes of large, waxy flowers in shades of green, yellow, pink, red, burgundy and white, often speckled or marked with a contrasting color. The elliptical petals radiate from a differently colored, prominent, three-lobed center. The tall flower spikes emerge from the base along with long, narrow, strap-like foliage. Miniature hybrids are especially beautiful and require less space.

Dendrobium orchids are sympodial epiphytes—they bear flowers on short stalks

Above: *Phalaenopsis* hybrid

Above: *Dendrobium nobile*

in clusters or groups. The open or flat flowers are often fragrant and come in shades of white, pink and purple. The flowers emerge from a tall, stem-like pseudobulb.

Oncidium orchids are sympodial epiphytes with clusters of tiny flowers on tall, wiry stems that emerge from the base of a pseudobulb. The brightly colored, large-lipped flowers are available in red, white, pink, yellow, brown and green, often with speckled markings.

Phalaenopsis hybrids (moth orchids) are monopodial epiphytes, meaning they produce a single stem from the roots at the base with no pseudobulb. Tongue-like, leathery leaves are produced from the base. Flat-faced flowers in pale-colored combinations of cream, green, pink and red emerge on arching stems.

Problems & Pests
Aphids, mealybugs, red spider mites and viruses, including *Cymbidium* mosaic virus. This virus cannot be treated so prevention is key. Sterilize all cutting tools.

Orchid flowers vary in size, shape and color but always have three sepals, two petals and one lip. The lower lip or petal is almost always a different shape and color from the others.

180

Ornamental Pepper

Capsicum

Features: colorful, fiery fruit **Height:** 6–12" (15–30 cm)
Spread: 8–10" (20–25 cm)

A colorful addition to a sometimes dreary fall and winter environment, ornamental pepper is a bit of an anomaly because it's grown for its ornamental fruit rather than its flowers or foliage. Without flowers or fruit, this plant is rather plain. The blooms, which emerge in late summer or fall, are followed by green, rounded or cone-shaped fruits that evolve into brightly colored 'ornaments' in fiery shades. The fruit will remain on the plant, in the right conditions, for at least two to three months. Ornamental pepper becomes available in fall, sometimes under the name Christmas pepper.

Growing

Ornamental pepper prefers **bright, direct sunlight**. The **soil-less mix** should be kept **moist** at all times. Mist the foliage often. Cool or average temperatures are best, with a minimum winter temperature of 55° F/13° C.

Tips

Hot, dry air is detrimental to ornamental peppers. Watch for signs of shrivelled and dropping foliage and fruit. Misting will prevent the onset of a spider mite infestation. Ornamental pepper is difficult to propagate, so it is not recommended. Although considered a short-term decorative plant, it can be kept for two to three years when the right conditions are present. Place it outdoors in the summer to ensure pollination when in flower. • The juice from the fruit is a powerful irritant. Keep the plant out of reach of both children and pets, and do not consume the fruit, which is purely ornamental.

Recommended

C. annuum produces 4" (10 cm) long, oval leaves on thin stems in a dense, bushy form. Small, inconspicuous, white flowers are followed by colorful cone-shaped or round, upright fruit in shades of yellow, red and orange. There are varieties available with speckled or mottled fruit as well. **'Christmas Greeting'** has 1" (2.5 cm) long fruit and **'Fiesta'** has 2" (5.1 cm) long fruit. **'Fireball'** produces round, cream-colored fruit

that changes to orange, then to scarlet red on a compact plant. **'Holiday Cheer'** has round fruit that evolves from cream to yellow, then purple to holly red. **'Red Missile'** has large, tapered fruit in brilliant shades of red, and **'Variegated Flash'** bears purple fruit.

Problems & Pests

Red spider mites are problematic in dry and hot conditions.

Ornamental peppers are often discarded after the fruit has fallen.

All photos: *C. annuum*

Paper Flower

Bougainvillea

Features: papery, colorful flowers on long, twining stems
Height: 10–15' (3–4.6 m) **Spread:** depends on support

Paper flower can be trained indoors with wire hoops or topiary supports to maintain a bushy form.

Paper flower is an exotic true tropical in its native Brazil, where it grows under the canopy of large rainforest trees. When grown as an indoor plant, it is prized for its colorful, papery bracts rather than its actual flowers, which are insignificant. This plant produces stems vigorously and will bloom prolifically from spring to summer in the right conditions. Paper flower benefits from a month or more outside in summer.

Above left: *B. x buttiana*; right & below: *B. x b.* 'California Gold'

Growing

Paper flower prefers **bright light** with a minimum of **four hours of direct sunlight daily.** Keep the **soil-based mix moist** from spring to summer, but let it almost dry out during winter until new growth appears. Mist the foliage occasionally. Normal room temperatures are best, with a minimum winter temperature of 50° F/10° C.

Tips

Prune paper flower back by at least one-third in fall and reduce watering. Keep the plant cool through winter and slowly increase the temperature, frequency and quantity of water in spring once new growth emerges. Repot in spring only if necessary. Propagate by stem cuttings in summer. The flowering is best if new growth is twisted around established stems and tied in for support.

Recommended

B. x buttiana can reach 20' (6.1 m) heights or more. It bears 1" (2.5 cm) wide pink or purple, papery bracts and narrow, smooth leaves. The foliage is produced on woody, spiny stems. This hybrid is less vigorous than *B. glabra.* 'California Gold' has peachy yellow bracts and 'Jamaica Red' has crimson bracts. 'Killie Campbell' and 'Orange King' have gold and orange bracts, and 'Surprise' has rose purple or white bracts or a combination of the two.

Opposite: *B. glabra* 'Variegata'

B. glabra (paper flower) is a basic species and less popular than the hybrids. It produces strong, twining branches with smooth, narrow, 3" (7.6 cm) long leaves. The branches are armed with vicious barbs. The colorful, papery bracts are borne on a bushy, 15' (4.6 m) tall form. 'Alexandra' bears pink flowers and is one of the most prolific bloomers, and 'Variegata' has cream-edged leaves with pink-purple flowers.

Problems & Pests

Aphids, red spider mites and mealybugs

Parlor Palm

Chamaedorea

Features: lush fronds and beautiful form **Height:** 4–5' (1.2–1.5 m)
Spread: 24–36" (61–91 cm)

*Parlor palm is also
known as good luck
palm and dwarf
mountain palm.*

There are more than 100 species of parlor palm, but only one is widely grown as a houseplant. It is popular because of its compact size and undemanding character. Its graceful appearance suits just about any décor or setting, it's easy to grow and lasts for years. Although compact, parlor palm is vertical in form and is often displayed as a specimen because its impact can be lost when it's grouped with other plants. It is an ideal plant for high traffic areas, including hallways and foyers, because it can tolerate some neglect.

Growing

Parlor palm prefers **moderate to bright light,** but avoid exposing it to direct sunlight. Supplement the **soil-based mix** with **peat moss** and **water generously** during the active growth period. Keep just moist during winter. Mist the foliage occasionally year-round. Normal room temperatures are best, with a minimum winter temperature of 55°–60° F/12°–15° C.

Parlor palm with black prince fig & coffee plant

Tips

Young plants are ideal for a terrarium. As they mature and outgrow the terrarium, transfer plants into their own container and display them in groupings until they're large enough to display on their own. Avoid high temperatures during winter because parlor palm benefits from a rest period. Repot only when the roots begin to grow through the drainage holes or bottom of the pot. Propagate by seed or division. • All parts are poisonous if ingested, and handling the plant may cause skin irritation.

Recommended

C. elegans (*Neanthe elegans*) produces bright green, arching fronds from the base. The leaves can reach 24" (61 cm) lengths and are comb-like in appearance. A short trunk develops with

maturity, but overall it remains small and compact. Sprays of tiny, yellow, ball-shaped flowers may appear on plants as young as three to four years but are insignificant.

Problems & Pests

Spider mite

All photos: *C. elegans*

Passion Flower

Passiflora

Features: exotic, colorful flowers borne on twining stems with attractive foliage **Height:** 16–20' (4.9–6.1 m) **Spread:** depends on support

Passion flower is one of my personal favorites. I've grown them for years on a balcony during the summer months, then brought them indoors from fall to spring. Passion flower blooms indoors and outside when placed in the right location. It bears quite unusual and exotic flowers, is a rampant climber and even has decorative foliage. A number of passion flowers are available, but most are difficult to find other than the most common species, *P. caerulea*. The fascinating flowers are intricately structured into tiers of different shapes, colors and forms, and you will feel compelled to closely inspect them as they unfold. They're produced along twining stems, opening one at a time per stem and remaining open for only one or two days each.

Growing

Passion flower requires **bright, indirect sunlight**. The **soil-based mix** should be kept **moist** at all times, but watered less during winter. Mist occasionally and provide a location with average warmth and a minimum temperature of 55° F in the winter. Do not exceed 70° F in the summer. Passion flower also requires good ventilation.

Tips

Cut the stems of a younger plant down to 9–12" (23–30 cm) in the spring. Prune the side branches of an older plant down to 3–4" (7.6–10 cm) and the main stems back by half to maintain its form. Propagate by stem cuttings in summer and sow seeds in spring. Repot annually in spring. • All parts are poisonous if ingested, especially the seeds.

Jesuit missionaries discovered passion flower in Brazil in the 18th century. They likened its white petals and sepals to ten witnesses of Christ's crucifixion, its anthers to five wounds to Christ's body, the rays of the corona of filaments to Christ's crown of thorns and the three stigmas to the nails that pinned Christ to the cross.

Recommended

P. caerulea bears twining stems with deeply lobed, 4" (10 cm) wide, pointed leaves and curly tendrils. Ornate 3" (7.6 cm) wide flowers are borne almost all summer long. The flowers have five greenish white petals, five white sepals and a ring of fine purple filaments surrounding prominent gold anthers. 'Constance Elliott' has white flowers.

Problems & Pests

Red spider mites

Passion flower is native to tropical locations in Brazil and Argentina. In its native habitat, it clings to the trunks of trees with its tendrils.

Opposite, top & right: *P. caerulea*

Peace Lily

Spathiphyllum

Features: white flowers and large, semi-glossy leaves
Height: 12"–4' (30 cm–1.2 m) **Spread:** 12–36" (30–91 cm)

Peace lily is a versatile plant suitable for a variety of settings and environmental conditions. The flowers are just an added bonus because the plant's foliage and form alone make the plant worthwhile. *Spathiphyllum* is a genus of about 35 species, but the hybrids available increase every year just to keep it interesting. Peace lily is more tolerant of lower light levels than other plants, is easy to care for and has the ability to clean indoor air of toxins.

Inset: *S.* x 'Lynise'; below: *S. wallisii*

Growing

Peace lily requires the **best possible light in winter** and **partial shade in summer,** out of direct sunlight. Keep the **soil-less mix consistently moist** from spring to fall, but water less during winter. It prefers higher humidity levels, so mist occasionally or use pebble trays. Peace lily is known for wilting when it has been underwatered. It will spring back from this state, if watered thoroughly. Normal room temperatures are fine, with a minimum winter temperature of 60° F/16° C. Place it in a location free of cold drafts.

Tips

Peace lily is a little sensitive to dry air. Higher humidity levels will benefit the health of the plant and will ward off spider mite attacks. Remove spent flower stems from the base where they emerge rather than just removing the flower itself. Propagate by division when repotting annually in spring. • Leaves are poisonous if ingested.

Recommended

S. floribundum grows 24"–4' (61 cm–1.2 m) tall and wide with dark green, strongly veined, spear-shaped leaves on round stems. White flowers tower above the foliage on tall, green stems. 'Mauna Loa,' perhaps the most well-known peace lily, is a vigorous cultivar with long leaves and large, fragrant flowers. 'Silver Streak' is medium sized with glossy leaves featuring a feather-like, creamy white pattern. The small flowers are numerous and creamy white.

S. wallisii grows 12–18" (30–46 cm) tall and produces 6–10" (15–25 cm) long, pointed leaves on rounded, tall stems. The leaves arch slightly at the leaf base, allowing the flowers to be seen better. Each flower is made up of a leaf-like,

white spathe that serves as the backdrop for a central white spadix covered in little nubs. Flowers change from greenish white to crisp white, then fade to a creamy white once spent.

S. x 'Cupido' has superb uniformity and long, wide leaves. It flowers easily and freely. It has a vigorous growth rate and produces lots of flowers.

S. x 'Lynise' grows 36" (91 cm) tall and wide. It is a larger, durable, proven variety with dense growth and continuous blooms.

S. x 'Petite' is a dwarf variety with narrow leaves and medium-sized flowers.

S. x 'Sensation' is the largest of all the peace lilies, reaching 3 1/2–4' (1.1–1.2 m) with tough, ribbed foliage and well-shaped flowers.

Problems & Pests

Red spider mites, whitefly, mealybugs, thrips, blight and root rot

Above: *S. wallisii*; right: *S.* x 'Lynise'

Peperomia

Peperomia

Features: textured and patterned foliage and spiky flowers
Height: 8–12" (20–30 cm) **Length:** trailing varieties can grow 24–36"
(61–91 cm) **Spread:** 8"–4' (20 cm–1.2 m)

The unusual flowers make a graceful addition to bushy peperomia varieties.

There are over 3000 existing species of peperomia, not including the cultivars. The upright and bushy peperomias are far more popular than the trailing types, but they're all fascinating. They vary in leaf texture, color, size and form. Serious peperomia collectors are as avid as orchid and African violet enthusiasts. I can't remember a time when I wasn't growing plants from this group, and I get just as excited when I find a new variety as I was years ago with the first one I grew.

Growing

Peperomia prefers **moderate to bright light** away from direct sunlight. Peperomias also thrive under **florescent light**. Variegated types require brighter

conditions than those with plain leaves. Keep the **peat moss–based mix just moist** by allowing the top half of the soil to dry out before each watering; water less in winter. High humidity is a must. Mist frequently and place the pot atop a pebble tray. Normal room temperatures are best, with a minimum winter temperature of 60° F/16° C.

Opposite & right: *P. caperata*

Tips

Peperomias are great for dish and bottle gardens and groupings. They have a little more impact when they're displayed together since they remain quite small and share similar conditions. Pinch the

Below: *P. magnoliifolia*

tips of the trailing types back in spring to encourage new and bushy growth. Repot only when necessary, and propagate by leaf or stem cuttings in spring. Peperomias are often killed with kindness by overwatering. Blackened lower leaves and stems, and corky swellings on the undersides of the foliage, are the usual signs of too much water.

Recommended

P. caperata (emerald ripple) produces heart-shaped, deep green leaves on long, red stems. The leaves are deeply veined and coarsely textured. Creamy white, spiky, upright flowers emerge through the foliage on red-tinged stems. It can grow to 10" (25 cm) tall. '**Emerald Ripple**' is a compact form of the species, and '**Little Fantasy**' is a dwarf variety. '**Variegata**' has green leaves with irregular, creamy white variegations along the leaf edge.

P. griseo-argentea (ivy-leaf pepper, silver-leaf pepper, platinum pepper) bears larger leaves than *P. caperata*. The silver leaves have green veins and are coarsely textured. Spiky flowers emerge through the foliage and are held vertically above the foliage on reddish stems.

P. magnoliifolia (desert privet) is a 8–10" (20–25 cm) tall, shrubby plant with branching stems that support rounded, glossy green leaves. 'Variegata' leaves are waxy and green with wide, irregular bands of creamy white along the leaf edges. The leaves are carried alternately along the fleshy, red-tinted stems.

P. scandens (P. serpens, cupid peperomia) is a trailing species with tiny, heart-shaped, 2" (5.1 cm) long leaves. The leaves are carried alternately on pink-tinged stems that can trail up to 4' (1.2 m). The leaves are smooth and waxy. Flowers are rarely produced in pots. 'Variegata' is the cultivar often found instead of the species. The green leaves are variegated with a creamy edge.

P. prostrata (creeping peperomia) produces tiny, heart-shaped leaves with silver and bronze markings. The leaves are alternately produced on red stems.

Above: *P. caperata*

Edema, which causes bulbous swellings on the undersides of the leaves, is the result of overwatering.

Philodendron

Philodendron

Features: foliage, form and easy care
Height: 6–15' (1.8–4.6 m) but depends on support
Length: trailing varieties can grow 4–6' (1.2–4.6 m)
Spread: 6–15' (1.8–4.6 m) but depends on support

Although most of the species recommended are climbers and may reach ceiling height, many are relatively slow growing and will produce less than 1" (2.5 cm) of new growth annually.

P hilodendrons are a beautiful, diverse group that includes climbing and non-climbing varieties. The climbing types require some form of support, the size of which determines how tall and wide they will grow. The non-climbing types are more structured and may spread to 8' (2.4 m) or more, but they can be contained by careful and selective pruning. Philodendrons are available in an interesting variety of leaf shapes and surfaces, often with stems, veins and margins in contrasting colors. I usually suggest philodendron if asked to recommend a hardy, maintenance-free and adaptable houseplant. Besides being almost impossible to kill, lasting for years and requiring little care or maintenance, philodendron is easy to display and a feast for the eyes.

Growing

Philodendron prefers **moderate to bright light** with no direct sunlight. The **soil-based mix** with added **peat moss** should be kept **consistently moist** during the growing season but watered less in winter. Keep the air moist in summer, and try humidifiers, pebble trays and misting to moisten the air in winter. Average warmth is best, with a minimum winter temperature of 55°–60° F/13°–16° C.

Opposite: *P. bipinnatifidum*
Above: *P. b.* 'Miniature Selloum'
Right: *P. scandens*

This page: *P. erubescens* cultivars

climbing types will require a strong structure for support, including moss poles, heavy stakes or wire forms. *P. scandens* can be allowed to trail freely over the edge of the pot, or it can be trained vertically on a small trellis or wire topiary form. Repot every two to three years in the spring. Propagate the climbing types with stem cuttings or air layering in summer. Non-climbing types can be propagated from shoots cut from the base of the stem. The non-climbing types can grow quite large and will require an adequate space to mature as specimens. The smaller climbing types can be displayed in hanging baskets or trained on a vertical support and displayed as specimens or in groupings. • All parts can be poisonous if ingested and mild skin irritations can occur with repeated contact with foliage.

P. scandens can tolerate cooler temperatures (minimum 50° F/10° C) and *P. melanochrysum* requires higher than average temperatures (minimum 65° F/ 18° C).

Tips

Grooming consists of cleaning the leaves with a damp cloth. The larger

Recommended

P. bipennifolium (fiddleleaf philodendron, horsehead philodendron, panda plant) is a climber with deeply lobed, arrowhead-shaped, mature leaves. The leathery leaves can grow to 12–32" (30–81 cm) long. Mature height and spread depend on the size of the support structure. 'Splash Gordon' has cream-splashed leaves.

P. bipinnatifidum (tree philodendron) is a non-climbing species that grows upright and reaches 4' (1.2 m) tall. The deeply lobed, heart-shaped leaves can grow 18" (46 cm) long on 18–24" (46–61 cm) long stems. This sturdy, spreading philodendron eventually forms a short trunk to support its 6' (1.8 m) spread. As the plant matures, the leaves become more deeply cut or indented. 'Miniature Sel-loum' is a dwarf variety with smaller leaves and overall form, and 'Variega-tum' has marbled, light green to yellow leaves and cream-streaked leaf stems.

P. erubescens (blushing philodendron) is a climbing variety that can grow to 6' (1.8 m). The dark green leaves are edged in red with purple leaf stalks and midribs. The large leaves are shaped like arrowheads with coppery under-sides. Its thick aerial roots should be carefully attached to a damp moss pole.

P. ilsemannii is another climber sport-ing green, heart-shaped leaves with creamy blotches.

P. melanochrysum (black gold philo-dendron, velour plant) is a climber with olive green, velvety leaves and detailed, creamy veins and midrib. The leaves can grow to 18–30" (46–76 cm) long. It produces insignificant flowers.

Above: *P. scandens*

P. scandens (heartleaf philodendron, sweetheart plant) is a climber that bears bronzy foliage that turns a deep green with age. The heart-shaped leaves have a shiny surface and are much smaller than other species with similarly shaped leaves. They are borne on green, wiry stems.

Problems & Pests
Aphids

Below: fiddle-leaf philodendron (far left) with weeping fig, black prince fig, aloe & Hawaiian schefflera

Piggyback Plant
Tolmiea

Features: piggyback foliage and form **Height:** 12–18" (30–46 cm)
Spread: 12–18" (30–46 cm)

Tolmiea was named after Dr. William Fraser Tolmie (1812–86) a surgeon at the Hudson's Bay Company depot at Fort Vancouver.

It's difficult not to stop and inspect piggyback plant because of its unique ability to produce new plantlets from the surface of an existing leaf. New leaves do appear to be carried on the 'backs' of more mature leaves, and eventually the plant forms a ball-shaped mound of layered foliage. *Tolmiea* is a genus of only one species, often grown in hanging baskets because the mature leaves get weighed down by newly produced foliage. Piggyback plant is also known as mother-of-thousands and youth-on-age. Its unique growth habit makes it a great teaching tool for adults and children.

Growing

Piggyback plant prefers **bright filtered light** with **some direct sunlight** but shade from intense midsummer sun. The **peat moss–** or **soil-based mix** should be kept **moderately moist** during the growing season but watered less in winter. Mist the foliage occasionally to deter red spider mite attacks. Cool room temperatures are best, with a minimum winter temperature of 55°–65° F/13°–18° C.

Tips

Cut back to encourage new growth from the base if the plant becomes too large and dense. Propagate by division or by removing plantlets from the leaves and rooting them for cuttings in spring.
• All parts can cause skin irritation with repeated contact.

Recommended

T. menziesii is a clump-forming plant with 4" (10 cm) long, heart-shaped hairy leaves with toothed edges. Small plantlets emerge where the leaf and stem join. Tiny, tubular, greenish flowers open along one side of the leaf. The green flowers are considered insignificant and aren't showy. 'Variegata' has yellow-splashed leaves, and 'Taff's Gold' bears both solid and variegated leaves.

Problems & Pests

Red spider mites

All photos: *T. menziesii*

Pilea
Pilea

Features: silver-patterned foliage and tolerance of poor conditions
Height: 6–12" (15–35 cm) **Spread:** 6–10" (15–25 cm)

Pilea is extremely popular, and for good reason—it grows in a variety of light locations and requires little care. I can't remember a time when I haven't owned one. Pilea was one of the first houseplants I experimented with, and the results were fantastic. I still have several new generations from cuttings I took from older plants. A terrarium garden is the perfect setting for this plant since it loves warmth and humidity. It looks great on its own and in groups, and because it is easy to grow, it's perfect for the novice indoor gardener.

Inset: *P. microphylla*; below: *P. cadierei*

Growing

Pilea prefers **moderate to bright, indirect sunlight**. Well-drained **loam** or **peat moss**–based potting mix is best. Keep it **evenly moist**, but allow the surface to dry out slightly between waterings during the growing season. Reduce the quantity or frequency of watering throughout winter. This plant requires warmth and will not tolerate temperatures below 55° F/12° C. Higher humidity levels are essential in drier regions.

Too much shade can cause discolored leaves with brown tips and edges.

Try to provide the best lit location to get the most attractive foliar coloration.

Tips

Pilea does best in a terrarium or bottle garden where it is warm and humid. Supplement humidity with a pebble tray or regular misting if the plant is grown in a pot. Pilea can become tall and thin over time, but pinching or shearing the newest growth or taking

Above: *P. microphylla*; right: *P. cadierei*

Above: *P. cadierei*; below: *P. involucrata*

cuttings can easily prevent this. The cuttings are best rooted directly in a moist potting medium with bottom heat. Ideally, stem tip cuttings should be taken and rooted in spring or summer. • All parts of pilea are poisonous if ingested. Keep these plants away from children and pets.

Recommended

P. cadierei (aluminum plant) is an upright, bushy plant that can reach 10–12" (30–35 cm) in height. Distinctly textured leaves are covered by four rows of silvery, raised patches between the veins, resulting in a quilted appearance. The newest growth and undersides are lightly tinged with red. Rounded, ball-shaped flowers are produced but are considered insignificant. **'Minima'** is a dwarf variety that grows 6" (15 cm) tall with smaller leaves.

P. involucrata (panamiga, friendship plant) is a trailing species, bearing round-tipped, bronze-green foliage. It grows 6–12" (15–30 cm) tall and has tiny, green, inconspicuous flowers. '**Moon Valley**' has deeply quilted leaves with brown veins. '**Norfolk**' has pink-tinged, metallic foliage.

P. microphylla (artillery plant) is an upright species and very new on the market. It produces tiny, round leaves on fleshy, branched stems. It can grow to approximately 24" (61 cm) in the right conditions.

Above: *P. cadierei*

Problems & Pests
Red spider mites and aphids

Sudden drops in temperature and wet compost can cause serious leaf drop.

Plush Vine

Mikania

Features: lacy purple foliage and trailing form **Height:** 3–4' (91 cm–1.2 m)
Length: trailing stems can reach 4' (1.2 m) **Spread:** depends on the pot width

Plush vine is one of my new experiments. I've always admired its beautifully intricate foliage, and now I have one hanging below a purple heart
(*Setcreasea pallida*) in a two-tiered hanging basket. Plush vine's lacy, green,
fuzzy leaves complement purple heart's long, trailing, purple stems very well.
Plush vine appears to be very delicate, which can be deceiving because this
plant is a vigorous and tough little creature. While it is most commonly
grown in hanging baskets, it can also be displayed on a pedestal or trained to
grow vertically on a structured support. Small, pale yellow flowers appear in
summer and contrast nicely with the ornate foliage.

Growing

Plush vine prefers **bright light** with **some direct sunlight**. The **soil-based mix** should be kept **moist** at all times but watered less in winter. This plant benefits from the occasional misting, but use a very fine spray of tepid water, and mist only in the evening to prevent the wet foliage from scorching in the hot sun. Plush vine enjoys average warmth, with a minimum winter temperature of 50°–55° F/10°–13° C.

Plush vine is native to tropical America, the West Indies and South Africa.

Tips

Repot if necessary in the spring and propagate by stem cuttings at the same time.

Mikania was named after Joseph Gottfried Mikan (1783–1814), a professor of botany in Prague, or possibly his son Johann Christian, who collected plants in Brazil and followed in his father's professional footsteps.

Recommended

M. dentata (*M. ternata*) produces leaves made up of three leaflets, known as palmate leaves. Wiry, purple stems covered in fine, purple hairs carry the paired leaflets along opposite sides of the stem. The dark green leaves are also covered in fine, purple hairs, creating a special effect shared by few others. The leaves are 1–2" (2.5–2.1 cm) long and more densely covered on the undersides than the upper surface.

Problems & Pests

Red spider mites, whiteflies and rust

All photos: *M. dentata*

Polka Dot Plant

Hypoestes

Features: boldly patterned and variegated foliage
Height: 24" (61 cm) **Spread:** 12–18" (30–46 cm)

Hypoestes is from the Greek hypo, under, and estia, house, an imaginative reference to the way the floral calyces are covered by bracts.

Polka dot plant is also known by a number of descriptive common names, including the measles plant, the flamingo plant, freckle face and pink dot. The pink and white, variegated leaves may be covered in dot-like markings or mottled with color. Polka dot plant is available in a variety of patterns and sizes and in shades of pink, red and white. This plant can grow larger, but usually it remains smaller in a home environment. Solitary lilac flowers are seldom produced but make a colorful addition to this already whimsical plant. Children love polka dot plant and it's easy enough for kids of any age to grow.

Above left: 'White Splash'; right: 'Rose Splash'

Growing

Polka dot plant requires a **bright location** with **some direct sunlight** to maintain vivid coloration, but protect it from the hot summer sun by filtering the light a little. The **soil-less mix** should be kept **evenly moist** from spring to fall and watered less in winter. Mist the leaves frequently in a room with average warmth. The minimum winter temperature should be no less than 55° F/13° C.

Tips

The leaves may revert to solid green when placed in poor light. Provide adequate light to maintain the best color and to prevent it from becoming straggly. Repot annually in spring, but only if necessary. Propagate by seed or stem cuttings in spring or summer. When you initially purchase a polka dot plant, it will be compact and stocky because of growth-regulating chemicals that are applied by the grower. The plant will eventually outgrow this stage and become leggy. Prevent legginess by pruning and providing adequate sunlight.

Recommended

H. phyllostachya produces slender stems that carry dark green, spotted rose to pale lavender, 2" (5.1 cm) long, oval leaves with pointed tips. The stems will eventually become woody at the base. It's rare that you would come across the species. The cultivars are far more popular and available, including '**Splash**,' which is larger and showier than the species and has pink spots. '**Rose Splash**' has darker pink leaves and '**White Splash**' has white markings.

Opposite: *P. phyllostachya*; right: 'Splash'

Ponytail Palm

Beaucarnea

Features: curly foliage from a swollen bulb **Height:** 3–4' (91 cm–1.2 m)
Spread: 12–36" (30–91 cm)

Ponytail palm is the most unusual of plants and not really a palm at all. It is really a bizarre-looking succulent with a swollen bulb that stores water for a base. That is why it can tolerate periods of dryness and won't tolerate excessive watering. It features a plume of green ribbons that arise from the center of the stem above a swollen, brown base. The leaves grow into long, narrow, grass-like blades that twist and curl, cascading right to the floor. If nothing else, ponytail palm is a conversation piece that requires little care and space. It will lend a delicate vertical element to just about any setting.

Growing

Ponytail palm prefers **bright light** with **some direct sunlight.** Supplement the **soil-based mix** with **leaf mold, peat moss** and **sand.** The mix should be **well drained** and **watered thoroughly** but allowed to become moderately dry before watering again. It is crucial not to overwater this plant because it is very prone to rot. It prefers average warmth, with a minimum of 50° F/10° C in winter.

Tips

This curious-looking plant is ideal for a modern or contemporary interior. It makes a stunning specimen because its growth habit makes its special features easy to see and appreciate. Repot every two to three years and only if necessary. Always provide good drainage, and always keep it in a pot relatively small for its age and size. Propagate by planting offsets when repotting—this can be a difficult process, so it is sometimes easier just to purchase an additional plant. If overwatered, stand the pot on dry newspaper for one to two days, changing the paper once it becomes saturated. Do not water the plant again until the top of the mix has dried out.

This plant thrives in locations with low humidity, similar to the air in most Canadian homes.

Recommended

B. recurvata produces 3–5' (91cm–1.5 m) long, narrow, arching leaves from a bulbous base that is partially exposed. The leaf edges are razor sharp. New growth emerges from the central stem.

Problems & Pests

Scale insects and red spider mites

All photos: *B. recurvata*

Prayer Plant

Maranta

Features: colorful and patterned foliage
Height: 10–12" (25–30 cm)
Spread: 10–12" (25–30 cm)

*Maranta was named after
B. Maranti, a 16th-century
Venetian botanist.*

This decorative plant is called prayer plant because its leaves fold together at night like hands brought together in prayer. The leaves will also fold up against drafts, excessive heat or cold and even intense light. Most plants from the *Maranta* genus move spontaneously when you least expect it, and change their arrangement from one hour to the next. Prayer plant does produce tiny, white flowers, but its beautiful, brightly marked leaves are the star attraction.

Above: *M. leuconeura*

Growing

Prayer plant prefers **moderate light** during the growing season and **bright, filtered light** in winter. The **soil-based mix** should be **watered thoroughly** but allowed to dry out slightly between waterings. Do not let it dry out completely. It thrives in high humidity and normal room temperatures, up to 75° F/24° C, with a minimum winter temperature of 60°–65° F/16°–18° C.

Tips

Grow prayer plant as a specimen or group it with other plants as an accent. It can also be trained up a short moss pole or trellis. Groom it by dusting it with a soft, dry cloth or soft duster to avoid damaging the satiny surface of the leaves. Repot in spring but only when the roots grow through the drainage holes, usually every other year. This plant prefers a shallow pot or an azalea pot because of its shallow root system. Propagate by division in spring, or cuttings in summer.

Opposite & right: *M. l.* var. *erythroneura*

Recommended

M. leuconeura (prayer plant, ten commandments) is a low-growing, spreading plant with large, elliptical leaves. The leaves are dark green with gray or maroon veins and burgundy undersides. *M. l.* var. *erythroneura* (herringbone plant) has shiny, pale green, satiny leaves with bright red veins and irregular green patches behind the midrib. *M. l.* var. *kerchoveana* (rabbit's foot, rabbit tracks) has gray-green leaves with a row of olive-colored spots on each side of the central midrib. *M. l.* var. *leuconeura* has broad, dark green leaves with a pale, comb-like pattern of silver veins and a velvety surface. 'Massangena' has blue-tinted leaves with rusty brown centers. A jagged band of silver runs along the midrib and silver lines run along the lateral veins.

Problems & Pests

Red spider mites

Rosary Vine

Ceropegia

Features: widely spaced, succulent, speckled foliage on thread-like stems, tubular flowers **Height:** 1" (2.5 cm) taller than the container **Length:** stems can reach 36" (91 cm) **Spread:** 2–3" (5.1–7.6 cm)

This fascinating succulent, trailing plant is not always easy to find, but it's well worth the search. Rosary vine is also commonly known as string of hearts, which aptly describes the shape of the foliage and how it's displayed. Rosary vine looks a little unusual for a trailing plant, and very similar to

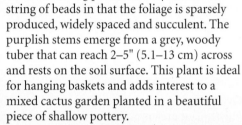

string of beads in that the foliage is sparsely produced, widely spaced and succulent. The purplish stems emerge from a grey, woody tuber that can reach 2–5" (5.1–13 cm) across and rests on the soil surface. This plant is ideal for hanging baskets and adds interest to a mixed cactus garden planted in a beautiful piece of shallow pottery.

Growing

Rosary vine prefers **bright light** with at least **four to five hours of direct sunlight** daily. The **soil-based mix** with added **sand** or **perlite** should be **well drained** and kept **moderately moist** during its active growth cycle, but watered less from fall to early spring. Tolerant of drier air, rosary vine prefers normal room temperatures, with a minimum winter temperature of 55° F/13° C.

Tips

Repot in early spring and propagate by stem cuttings. Remove stem tubers from the plant and place them around the perimeter of a new container as another means of propagation. Rosary vine requires a bright location; otherwise, the foliage will fade and leaves will emerge even further apart than normal on the thread-like stems.

Recommended

C. linearis spp. *woodii* (hearts entangled, sweetheart vine, hearts on a string, *C. woodii*) produces slender, thread-like, purplish stems. The twining stems emerge from a grey tuber. Fleshy, heart-shaped, succulent leaves are produced in pairs, widely spaced from base to tip. The leaves have a pale grey-green speckled surface with lavender-grey undersides. Inconspicuous, pinkish, tubular flowers are produced in summer, sometimes followed by small, creamy colored tuberous growths.

Problems & Pests

Whitefly may affect the newest growth.

All photos: *C. l.* spp. *woodii*

Rose of China

Hibiscus

Features: large, colorful flowers and form **Height:** 6' (1.8 m)
Spread: 12–36" (30–91 cm)

R ose of China is an extremely popular flowering houseplant that easily adapts to life outdoors during the summer months. *Hibiscus* is a genus of 250–300 species of annuals, perennials, shrubs and trees, but just two species are widely grown as indoor plants. *H. rosa-sinensis* and *H. schizopetalas* are both free-flowering shrubs best grown in a sun-filled room or conservatory. They're dense shrubs, clothed in deep, dark green foliage and brightly colored, exotic flowers that remain open for only one day. The flowers are short lived but are often produced in succession for long periods. This plant offers a lesson in appreciating what's in front of you before it's gone.

Growing

Rose of China prefers **bright light** with **short periods of direct sunlight** but not during the hottest part of the day.

The **soil-based mix** with added **peat moss** should be kept **consistently moist**; do not allow it to dry out. Mist the foliage occasionally in a room with average warmth. Allow the plant to rest during winter, with a minimum winter temperature of 60° F/16° C.

Tips

When displayed in small groupings, rose of China looks best as a shrub, but when using it as a specimen, a standard or tree form is better. Avoid turning or moving the plant once the buds have formed or they may drop. Remove the flowers once they are spent, and repot annually in spring. It can be placed outdoors in a sheltered location in summer. Cut the stems back by one-half to two-thirds in early spring to maintain a compact form, and shorten long shoots after flowering or late in winter. Propagate with cuttings in late spring to late summer.

Recommended

H. rosa-sinensis (rose of China) can grow to 6' (1.8 m) with 6" (15 cm) long, coarsely toothed leaves. The glossy, dark green leaves are oval in shape. Flowers 4–6" (10–15 cm) wide unfurl from tightly twisted buds, revealing prominent stamens. The flowers come in shades of red, orange, yellow, white, pink and apricot. There are single- and double-flowering varieties. 'Cooperi' has variegated foliage with red flowers and 'Koenig' bears flowers with a double ring of bright yellow petals and a central, red eye.

H. schizopetalus (Japanese hibiscus, Japanese lantern) is more graceful in appearance. It produces slender,

arching branches and drooping, pink flowers with fringed, reflexed petals. Each flower has a prominent stamen and can grow to 2" (5.1 cm) wide.

Problems & Pests

Red spider mites, scale insects, mealybugs, whitefly and aphids

All photos: *H. rosa-sinensis*

Silk Oak

Grevillea

Features: feathery foliage and form **Height:** 6' (1.8 m)
Spread: 24"–4' (60 cm–1.2 m)

This vigorously growing plant can be purchased when young and small and is often found in trays of mixed ferns at your local garden center. The feathery foliage may remind you of ferns, but silk oak is not a fern at all. The lacy foliage becomes less finely divided over time. Some consider silk oaks to be unattractive once mature, but I think they're just as interesting and beautiful, with a different appeal. They do flower when grown outdoors, or in their native habitat, but not in cultivation.

Growing

Silk oak prefers **bright filtered** or **direct sunlight.** It adapts easily to locations with partial shade. Keep the **soil-based mix moderately moist,** but water less in winter. This plant prefers increased humidity if grown in a warm room. Pebble trays and misting are a benefit. It tolerates a wide range of temperatures, with a minimum of 45°–50° F/7°–10° C in winter.

Tips

Silk oak is best grown in a container with other plants or in a terrarium. Good companion plants are *Peperomia* and *Maranta.* It looks best planted in a shallow bowl or container where the finely cut foliage can provide an interesting contrast. It also makes a great specimen plant, especially as it matures. Repot when the roots emerge through the drainage holes, in spring or summer, and propagate by seed or soft stem cuttings in spring or summer.

Silk oak does best in a rather cool room.

All photos: *G. robusta*

• All parts can cause skin irritation with repeated contact.

Recommended

G. robusta can reach 6' (1.8 m) in height, but most plants are much smaller. It bears finely divided leaves with a slightly downy surface and silky undersides.

Problems & Pests

Red spider mites

Silver Vine

Scindapsus

Features: silver marked foliage **Height:** 4–6" (10–15 cm) **Length:** trailers can reach lengths of up to 4' (1.2 m)

Silver vine is a plant with subtle markings and a trailing habit, ideal for training on vertical supports or left to cascade over the edge of a decorative container. *Scindapsus* represents about 40 evergreen climbers and was once a species included in the genus *Epipremnum* (devil's ivy). It is incredibly easy to grow, requires little care and effortlessly blends into many settings.

Growing

Silver vine requires **moderate to bright light** with **a few hours of direct sunlight**. The **soil-based mix** should be kept **consistently moist** throughout the growing season but let it dry slightly between waterings during winter. Mist the foliage often and place on a pebble tray to supplement humidity levels. It prefers average warmth, with a minimum winter temperature of 60° F/16° C.

Tips

Avoid all drafts and pinch out growing tips to encourage a bushy growth habit. Repot annually but only if necessary and propagate by stem cuttings in spring or summer.

Recommended

S. pictus '**Argyraeus**' (satin potho) produces leaves with a dull but silky surface marked with silver blotches or irregular dots. Each leaf is surrounded by a thin, silvery white line. The heart-shaped leaves are carried alternately on slender, wiry stems.

Scindapsus, *a name used in ancient Greece for plants resembling ivy, was later applied to this genus of climbing plants. All* Scindapsus *varieties produce aerial roots.*

All photos: *S. p. 'Argyraeus'*

Silvery Inch Plant

Tradescantia

Features: colorful, banded foliage **Height:** 6–8" (15–20 cm)
Length: stems can trail to 36" (91 cm) **Spread:** 10–24" (25–61 cm)

Silvery inch plant is a vigorous, trailing plant with showy, colorful foliage. This plant requires little care and is often found in hanging baskets because of its long, cascading stems clothed in glistening foliage. *Tradescantia* is a genus of approximately 70 species, including other plants often used as houseplants for their decorative, ornate foliage. Silvery inch plant is popular and somewhat common because of its versatility and decorative appearance.

Growing

Silvery inch plant requires a **bright, sunny location** but is tolerant of partial shade. The **peat moss–** or **soil-based mix** should be **moist** at all times, but reduce watering in winter to allow the surface to dry slightly between waterings. Mist the foliage occasionally and place in a room with average temperatures and a minimum winter temperature of 55° F/13° C.

Tips

Pinch off the growing tips regularly to encourage bushier growth. Use the pinched tips for propagating. The leaves and stems are delicate and are easily damaged when handled. Brown tips and margins are a sure sign that the plant is in a spot that is too dry and hot. The foliage may revert back to solid green or become dull if not provided with adequate sunlight. Repot only when rootbound. • The leaves can cause a mild skin irritation with repeated contact.

Recommended

T. zebrina has lance-shaped, 2" (5.1 cm) long leaves with a banded silver and green upper surface, a fine purple line along the edge and purple undersides. The leaves are produced alternately on creeping or trailing stems. Small white or pink-red flowers are produced. **'Purpusii'** (bronze inch plant) has deep green leaves flushed with purple and tiny purple-pink, three-petalled flowers. **'Quadricolor'** has silver-, green-, purple- and pink-striped leaves.

Problems & Pests

Red spider mites

It is important to find the perfect balance between overwatering and underwatering since silvery inch plant is often killed by one or the other.

All photos: *T. zebrina*

Snake Plant

Sansevieria

Features: upright, variegated foliage **Height:** 8"–5' **Spread:** 8"–24"

Snake plant's 60 species and untold number of varieties and cultivars can be divided into two classes. The bird's nest types are low growing, neat and form compact rosettes of foliage whereas the tall, upright types produce foliage that stands erect from the soil's surface. Snake plant is easy to care for and can tolerate poor conditions and a little neglect. It makes a great specimen plant for a space that needs a vertical element. This plant was also tested by NASA and proven to remove formaldehyde, benzene and carbon monoxide from the air.

Growing

Snake plant prefers **bright light** but can also tolerate lower light levels. The **soil-based mix** should be **watered moderately** during the growing season. Allow the top 1" (2.5 cm) of the mix to dry out between waterings. Water just enough during winter to prevent the mix from completely drying out.

Above: *S. trifasciata*

Avoid getting water into the center of the rosette of leaves to prevent rot. Average to warm temperatures are best, with a minimum winter temperature of 55° F/13° C.

Tips

Choose a weighty decorative container for larger specimens to provide stability for this top-heavy plant. Repotting is only necessary when the roots seem about to burst out of the pot. Propagate by division from late winter to early summer when repotting. Alternatively, separate offsets from the base of the plant using a sharp knife to cut through the rhizome and pot individually. • All parts can cause nausea if ingested and skin irritation with repeated contact.

Recommended

S. trifasciata is grown for its stiff, mottled, spear-like leaves that are sometimes variegated or marked with paler cross banding. It can reach 5' (1.5 m) in height but usually remains smaller indoors. A number of cultivars exist, including '**Golden Hahnii**' (golden bird's nest), which has leaves with broad yellow margins and stripes, and '**Hahnii**,' a low-growing, compact rosette with relatively broad leaves that grows to only 8" (20 cm) tall. '**Laurentii**' has fleshy leaves that form a rosette from a thick rhizome. The sword-shaped leaves are sharply pointed, stiff and very tall, up to 24" (61 cm). The leaves are dark green with horizontal bands of pale green that resemble snakeskin and golden yellow leaf margins. Rarely, this variety produces sprays of small, creamy white flowers. '**Silver Hahnii**' has dark green, mottled leaves.

Problems & Pests

Root and stem rot

All photos: 'Laurentii'

Spider Plant

Chlorophytum

Features: foliage, form and trailing plantlets **Height:** 12" (30 cm)
Length: trailing stems can reach 4' (1.2 cm)
Spread: 24–36" (61–91 cm)

Spider plants are incredibly adaptable. They'll tolerate dry air and grow in hot or cool temperatures and bright or shaded rooms.

Common names are often reflective of a plant's appearance, and spider plant is no exception. The grass-like, narrow leaf blades gracefully arch as they grow, creating a spider-like effect, and the long, trailing stems that cascade over the pot's edge carrying small plantlets resemble baby spiders dangling from silky threads. Spider plant isn't only attractive, it's beneficial as well because it removes toxins from the air we breathe. A NASA study found that spider plant removes formaldehyde molecules from indoor air. These molecules are released by such common things as foam insulation, pressed wood office furniture, flooring and even paper towels. This is one plant no one should be without, at home or at work.

Growing

Spider plant prefers **moderate to bright light** away from direct sunlight. The **soilless mix** should be kept **consistently moist** for the growing season and watered less in winter. Mist the foliage occasionally in summer and provide a location with average warmth, but no cooler than 45° F/7° C in winter.

Tips

Spider plant is known for pushing itself right out of its container over time. It produces thickened, white, rigid root sections that rapidly fill a container's bottom, elevating the rootball from its pot. Remove at least one-third of the thickened roots and repot when necessary. Propagate by pegging down the plantlets in moistened potting mix, then cut the stem once rooted. Alternatively, divide the mother plant at repotting time.

Recommended

C. comosum produces grass-like blades that arise from the center and gracefully arch over time, creating an arching rosette. The green- or white-striped leaves can reach 8–20" (20–51 cm) long. Flowering stems emerge from the rosette bearing tiny, white flowers followed by young plantlets. The stems are weighed down by the plantlets, causing them to become pendent. **'Mandaianum'** leaves grow 6" (15 cm) long with a yellow central stripe, and **'Milky Way'** has cream-edged leaves. **'Variegatum'** has cream to white leaf margins, and **'Vittatum'** has leaves with a white central stripe and green edges.

Problems & Pests

Aphids are an occasional problem.

All photos: 'Vittatum'

Spineless Yucca

Yucca

Features: razor sharp foliage and woody stems
Height: 4–6' (1.2–1.8 m), varies with length of the prepared 'trunk'
Spread: 12–36" (30–91 cm)

Spineless yuccas are native to Mexico.

There are two distinct types of spineless yucca. The 'stick' yucca that has a stocky, woody trunk from which two or more rosette sprouts emerge, and the 'tip' yucca, which is stemless and consists of just one rosette of leaves. The prepared stick is usually imported from South America and forced to produce foliage. Both types are great architectural plants ideal for use as specimens. They're easy to grow, tolerate dry air, require little care or maintenance and are great plants for beginners.

Growing

Spineless yucca prefers **bright, direct sunlight** throughout the year. The **soil-based mix** should be kept **moist** and watered thoroughly during the growing season. In winter, let the soil dry out almost completely before watering again. Normal room temperatures are best, with a minimum winter temperature of 50° F/10° C.

Tips

Spineless yucca benefits from being outdoors in summer, but only if kept in a sheltered, sunny location. Tall plants are top-heavy and prone to falling over when they're placed into a lightweight, decorative pot. Repot in spring but only when rootbound, and top dress annually when mature. Propagate by removing offsets and potting them separately.

Recommended

Y. elephantipes has a stout, woody trunk or cane with one to two foliar rosettes. The leaves are long, narrow and sword-shaped. They're pointed at the tips and have razor sharp edges. '**Jewel**' has faint, creamy yellow margins between green stripes. '**Silver Star**' has leaves with a silver streak that runs along each leaf center, and '**Variegata**' has green leaves with yellow variegation.

Problems & Pests

Red spider mites

All photos: *Y. elephantipes*

Spreading Clubmoss

Selaginella

Features: fern-like foliage and dormant state **Height:** 1–6" (2.5–15 cm)
Spread: 6–12" (15–30 cm)

Spreading clubmoss is best known for its ability to enter into a completely
dormant state by curling up during times of severe drought—a logical
adaptation considering it is native to arid areas. When the roots are immersed
in or make contact with water, the leaves quickly unfurl and come back to life
right before your eyes. *S. lepidophylla* is commonly known as the resurrection plant or rose of Jericho. It is said to have mystical qualities and return
good deeds when it is propagated with faith and love. If nothing else, spreading clubmoss is guaranteed to spark conversation.

S. lepidophylla
can easily
adapt to
going in
and out of
dormancy
time and
time again
without
fail.

Growing

Spreading clubmoss prefers **moderate light** or **partial shade**; avoid direct sunlight year-round. The **peat moss–based mix** with added **coarse sand** should be kept **moist** at all times. Reduce watering in winter to suit the lower temperatures. Provide as much humidity as possible by misting, pebble trays and grouping, or grow them in a terrarium. Average room temperatures are best, with a minimum winter temperature of 55° F/13° C.

Above & center: *S. lepidophylla*

Tips

Avoid drafty locations and hot sunny windows. Spreading clubmoss thrives in a moist, humid atmosphere like that found in a bottle garden or terrarium. If you don't opt for an enclosed setting, you can use a shallow pot or pan. Propagate by division or pot offsets separately. Cut the stems of *S. kraussiana* back by up to half in the spring to prevent the plant from becoming too large.

Below: *S. kraussiana* with *S. lepidophylla*

Recommended

S. kraussiana (spreading clubmoss) produces creeping stems with filigreed, green foliage. Individual stems can grow to 12" (30 cm) long, and they root readily as they spread over the surface of the potting mix. The tiny, bright green leaves look mossy and are carried on branching stems that quickly form a dense mat. 'Aurea' has yellow-tinged foliage.

S. lepidophylla (curiosity plant, resurrection plant, rose of Jericho) produces a rosette of green, fern-like foliage when out of its dormancy but turns brown, dries up and curls into a ball with exposed shallow roots when dormant. It can reach a width of 6–12" (15–30 cm) but grows to only 1–2" (2.5–5.1 cm) tall.

S. martensii is an upright plant with stems that grow to about 12" (30 cm) long. The tips later turn upwards and produce aerial roots. Variegated, feathery, green foliage is also available in varieties including 'Watsoniana,' which has silvery white tips.

Opposite & right: *S. kraussiana*

String-of-Beads
Senecio

Features: round, pea-like leaves on stringy stems **Height:** 1–2" (2.5–5.1 cm)
taller than the edge of the pot **Length:** trailing stems can reach 36" (91 cm)
Spread: 1–2" (2.5–5.1 cm) wider than the diameter of the pot

It's not difficult to visualize this plant when you hear its common name—it really does look like a string of beads or fresh peas. This succulent is part of a strange group of plants that all look vastly different from one another. This group includes German ivy (*S. mikanioides*) and cineraria (*S.* x *hybridus*). If you put them all together, you would never believe that they are related, but they are. String-of-beads foliage emerges in spring and lasts for months, and it's some of the most unique and strange-looking foliage around.

Growing

String-of-beads grows best in **bright light** with periods of direct sunlight, except in summer. A **well-drained, soil-based mix** is best, with added **coarse sand** to improve drainage. Keep **moist** during the growing season, but allow the surface to dry slightly between waterings, and water sparingly in winter. Warm locations are best, with a minimum winter temperature of 50° F/10° C.

Tips

String-of-beads is often found in hanging baskets to best display its unique growth and habit. The trailing stems can also be kept shorter or wound into a bunch and placed on top of the rootball for a massed effect.

Recommended

S. rowleyanus produces long, string-like stems that carry perfectly round, pea-like, succulent foliage in opposite pairs from base to tip. Small, white flowerheads resembling shaving brushes emerge in spring.

Problems & Pests

Aphids and spider mites may attack the new shoots.

String-of-beads is native to parts of Namibia and is included in the same genus as the annual bedding plant dusty miller.

The flowers exude an aroma reminiscent of cinnamon.

All photos: *S. rowleyanus*

Swedish Ivy

Plectranthus

Features: glossy foliage, form and delicate flowers **Height:** 12" (30 cm) **Length:** trailing stems can reach 3–4' (91 cm–1.2 m) **Spread:** 2–6" (5.1–15 cm) wider than the container

The sap exuded from cut or broken stems can stain just about anything it touches.

The common names for different species of Swedish ivy reflect their popularity in Scandinavia, but this plant is equally popular in Canada. Swedish ivy is known mostly for its glossy, thick foliage, delicate flowers and trailing form, but it does not really resemble ivy. It is easy to grow and propagate, tolerates the occasional drying out and suits any décor. *Plectranthus* species will also flourish in dry, indoor air where true ivies would fail.

Above: *P. oertendahlii*; center: *P. forsteri* 'Marginatus'

Growing

Swedish ivy prefers **bright light** or **partial shade**. Avoid direct sunlight. The **peat moss–based mix** should be kept **moist** at all times, but watered less in winter. Mist the leaves occasionally and provide average warmth and a minimum winter temperature of 50° F/10° C.

Tips

Swedish ivy is often planted in hanging baskets because of its trailing habit. It can also be grown in a tall, decorative pot or placed on a pedestal or plant stand to showcase its growth habit. Pinch out the stem tips from time to time to encourage a bushy growth habit. Use the tip cuttings for propagation. Keep the trailers trimmed back to a reasonable length to prevent it from becoming straggly. • The sap can cause mild skin irritations.

grow to 36" (91 cm) wide and 12–18" (30–46 cm) tall.

Problems & Pests

Mealybugs, red spider mites, leaf spot and root rot

Recommended

P. oertendahlii (Swedish ivy) has glossy, rounded leaves with scalloped edges. The fleshy leaves measure 1" (2.5 cm) across with white veins on the uppersides and purple undersides. Delicate, creamy white flowers with purple speckles are borne occasionally on fleshy, rounded stems.

P. forsteri (candle plant) is more upright, producing 2" (5.1 cm) wide leaves with a hairy surface and underside, and scalloped edges. '**Marginatus**' leaves are edged in creamy white. It can

Umbrella Tree

Schefflera

Features: large foliage and upright growth habit
Height: 6–8' (1.8–2.4 cm)
Spread: 4–6' (1.2–1.8 cm)

Umbrella tree varieties are easy to grow and prized for their tough foliage, which radiates from a point like the spokes of an umbrella.

Umbrella tree is one popular plant. Practically no home or workplace is without one. *Schefflera* is a large genus of evergreen shrubs

Above: *S. actinophylla*

and trees, a few of which are grown as specimen houseplants. Umbrella tree is a beautiful, upright, shrubby plant that can tolerate dry indoor air and is known to filter a variety of noxious gases from the air. It's available in solid green and variegated varieties and best displayed in an open space where it will have room to comfortably grow and mature.

Growing

Umbrella tree requires **medium to bright light** with no exposure to direct sunlight. The **peat moss–based mix** should be kept **consistently moist** throughout the growing season but watered less during winter. Mist the foliage regularly and place in a location with average warmth and a minimum winter temperature of 55° F/13° C.

Tips

Taller plants may require support as they grow. Moss poles or simple bamboo stakes are beneficial in this instance. Remove dust and debris from the foliage with a damp or dry, soft cloth. Pinch off the growing tips to encourage bushier growth and place larger plants in a weighty container to anchor the top-heavy growth. Propagate by cuttings in summer and repot when the roots begin to grow through the drainage holes. Avoid locations exposed to cold drafts. • The leaves can be poisonous if ingested, and the sap may cause skin irritation with repeated contact.

Recommended

S. actinophylla (Australian umbrella tree) is a bushy tree that can grow to ceiling height if left unchecked. The large, spreading, glossy leaves are composed of 5–16 leaflets, each of them about 4–8" (10–20 cm) long. This plant is shrubby when young but becomes less dense as it matures.

S. arboricola (Hawaiian schefflera) is an erect, well-branched shrub bearing leaves composed of 7–16 oval, glossy leaflets that radiate from the top of the leaf stalk like an umbrella. 'Aurea' has gold, variegated leaves.

Problems & Pests

Red spider mites, mealybugs and scale insects

Opposite, top right & right: *S. arboricola*

Velvet Plant

Gynura

Features: fuzzy purple foliage and trailing habit **Height:** 6–8" (15–20 cm)
Length: trailing stems can reach 3–4' (91 cm–1.2 m) lengths
Spread: 4–8" (10–20 cm) wider than container

Velvet plant is a vigorous grower and has no special needs. It produces spectacular, dark green foliage covered in shiny, dark purple hairs. When kept in a location with bright light, the color intensity increases, creating a stunning effect. The leaf shape is also very decorative, resembling a holly leaf with soft-toothed edges. Mature velvet plants are often found in hanging baskets to best exhibit their trailing habit and ornate foliage and stems. Kids love this plant, not only for its color but because its soft and fuzzy leaves invite touching. Orange-yellow flowers are produced but should be removed because of their unpleasant odor.

Growing

Velvet plant is best grown in **bright light** with **some direct sunlight**. The **soil-** or **peat moss–based mix** should be kept **moist** at all times but watered less in winter. Increase humidity levels with pebble trays and humidifiers. Avoid wetting the hairy leaves because the hairs can trap water, causing rot. Average warmth is best, with a minimum winter temperature of 60° F/16° C.

Tips

Pinch the new growing tips out occasionally to encourage bushy growth. Propagate by stem cuttings in the spring and repot annually, but only if necessary.

Recommended

G. aurantiaca (*G. sarmentosa*) produces 3" (7.6 cm) long, dark green, holly-like leaves. The leaves and stems are covered in fine, purple hairs that reflect light, so the entire leaf appears almost purple. The stems can grow to be quite long but should be pinched to maintain a reasonable length. '**Purple Passion**' produces toothed leaves on trailing or climbing stems. Both stems and leaves are covered in velvety, purple hairs.

The youngest foliage and newest shoot tips are often the hairiest and the most intensely colored, especially in bright light.

All photos: *G. aurantica*

Wandering Jew

Tradescantia

Features: patterned foliage and trailing growth habit **Height:** 4–6"
(10–15 cm) **Length:** trailing stems can grow 24–36" (61–91 cm) long
Spread: 4–6" (10–15 cm) wider than the container

The oval leaves of the *Tradescantia* species are easily identified by the way they are carried alternately on wiry but fleshy, trailing stems. They're available in a variety of color combinations and are rarely dull. Wandering Jew is a white, variegated variety that has been a popular houseplant for decades, if not centuries. *Tradescantia* varieties may bloom indoors, but it's the decorative foliage that will catch your attention because the flowers are rather insignificant.

Growing

Wandering Jew prefers **bright light** with **some direct sunlight**. Keep the **peat moss–based mix moderately moist** throughout the growing season, but water less in winter. Mist the leaves occasionally, or use a pebble tray to supplement humidity levels. Average warmth is best, with a minimum of 45°–50° F/7°–10° C.

Tips

Pinch out the growing tips regularly to encourage bushy growth, and remove all green shoots as soon as they appear. Propagate by stem cuttings and repot if necessary in spring, summer or fall. Trim the stems back if they begin to appear untidy or if the foliage browns or shrivels. • The leaves can cause a mild skin irritation with repeated contact.

Recommended

T. cerinthoides (flowering inch plant) has hairy, broad, fleshy leaves. Narrowly oval and 2–4" (5.1–10 cm) long, the leaves are produced in two distinct rows on hairy, trailing stems. Both leaves and flowers are usually suffused with purple. **'Variegata'** produces dull leaves with longitudinal, cream stripes and purple undersides. The stems are hairy and the flowers are pink with white bases.

T. fluminensis (wandering Jew) is a trailing plant with hairless stems carrying short-stalked, green or variegated leaves produced alternately from base to tip. The leaves are sometimes flushed purple underneath. **'Albovitatta'** (*T. albiflora* 'Albovitatta') has creamy, white-striped leaves; **'Quicksilver'**

has white-striped leaves; **'Tricolor Minima'** has smaller leaves, variegated with pink, white and green stripes and red undersides. Flowers are produced but are insignificant. **'Variegata'** has yellow- and white-striped leaves with pale purple undersides and small, white flowers.

Problems & Pests

Red spider mites

Above right: *T. fluminensis* 'Variegata'

Wax Plant

Hoya

Features: succulent foliage and waxy clusters of flowers **Height:** 4–6"
(10–15 cm) **Length:** trailing stems can reach 15' (4.6 m) lengths
Spread: 6–8" (15–20 cm) wider than container if let to trail

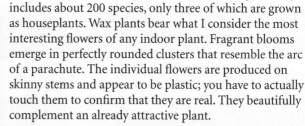

Wax plants are ideal for those with little experience and a new-found
fascination for indoor gardening. It's almost impossible to kill a wax
plant, and even with a little neglect, it will grow and bloom. The genus *Hoya*
includes about 200 species, only three of which are grown
as houseplants. Wax plants bear what I consider the most
interesting flowers of any indoor plant. Fragrant blooms
emerge in perfectly rounded clusters that resemble the arc
of a parachute. The individual flowers are produced on
skinny stems and appear to be plastic; you have to actually
touch them to confirm that they are real. They beautifully
complement an already attractive plant.

Inset: *H. carnosa*; below: *H. carnosa* 'Variegata'

Growing

Wax plants prefer **bright light** with **some direct sunlight**. The **well-drained, peat moss–based mix** should be **watered moderately** during the growing season but let to dry slightly between waterings. Water less in winter. Mist the leaves regularly but not when in bloom. Average to warm rooms are best, with a minimum winter temperature of 60° F/16° C.

Tips

Wax plants are often grown in hanging baskets but can also be trained to climb a vertical support such as a trellis, topiary form or hoop. Avoid disturbing wax plants once the buds appear, and don't remove spent flowers. Repotting isn't necessary until it's about to burst out of its container. Propagate by stem cuttings in spring. • The stems contain a white, milky sap that is poisonous.

Recommended

H. carnosa (wax plant) is a vigorous, twining plant with stems that can reach 15' (4.6 m) or more. The new stems are bare, but leaves do appear later. The fleshy leaves are solid green or green with white speckles. White to pale pink, fragrant, waxy flowers are produced once or twice a year. They're borne in clusters with darker centers. **'Exotica'** produces leaves with yellow centers and **'Krimson Princess'** has red-colored young foliage. **'Variegata'** bears green flowers with creamy edged leaves.

H. lanceolata spp. *bella* (miniature wax plant) produces 24" (61 cm) long, trailing stems that carry 1" (2.5 cm) long, almost triangular leaves with creamy white edges. The leaves are smaller than *H. carnosa*; however, the flower clusters are similar in size and appearance. This variety is a little more difficult to grow than *H. carnosa* because it prefers a little more heat and humidity, but less light.

Problems & Pests
Mealybugs

The flowers produce a sticky nectar that often forms on them in droplets.

This page: *H. carnosa* 'Variegata'

ZZ Plant

Zamioculcas

Features: foilage and tolerance to conditions
Height: 24"–4' (61 cm–1.2 m)
Spread: 36" (91 cm)

This prehistoric-looking plant may be a little expensive, but only because of its slower growth rate and relative rarity.

This is the newest, and I believe, one of the best houseplants available today for Canadian indoor gardeners. ZZ plant doesn't look like much else and stands out in a crowd. It is perfectly suited to our indoor conditions, adapting nicely to low light levels, dry, centrally heated homes and busy schedules. ZZ plant is also able to thrive with less moisture because of an underground, tuber-like potato that stores water. Its thick foliage and fleshy stems also have the ability to hold water. Though relatively new, this plant will become more available as gardeners discover its beauty and adaptability.

Growing

ZZ plant prefers **bright, filtered light to partial shade**. The **soil-based mix** should be kept **evenly moist** during the growing season. The top 1" (2.5 cm) of the mix should be allowed to dry to the touch between waterings. Water less during winter. Misting is beneficial but not necessary. This plant prefers temperatures up to 85° F/29° C during the day and 65°–75° F/18°–24° C at night. Minimum winter temperatures should not fall lower than 62° F/ 17° C.

Tips

ZZ plant will benefit from being placed outdoors in a partially shaded location during summer where it will thrive in the fresh air and dappled light. The only way to harm this plant is to overwater it. Repot only when it looks as if it will burst out of its pot, and propagate by seed or leaf cuttings using the leaflets. • All parts are poisonous if ingested.

All photos: *Z. zamiifolia*

Recommended

Z. zamiifolia produces leathery leaves on upright, fleshy stems with swollen bases. The waxy leaves are borne in opposite pairs and are especially glossy when young. The stems emerge from a thick, horizontal rhizome located just under the surface of the potting mix. In ideal conditions, short, white flowers emerge near the base of the foliage.

Other Plants to Consider

Amaryllis
Hippeastrum hybrida

Produces thick, rounded flower stalks, long, strap-like foliage and a ring of large, brightly colored, trumpet-shaped flowers from a bulb base that sits slightly above the soil. Flowers are solid, striped or flushed with another color. They can reach 24" (60 cm) in height and last up to four weeks.

Force bulbs a few months before Christmas by planting in a soil-based mix with the top third above the soil. Place in bright light with some direct sunlight. Water sparingly until a flower bud emerges, then increase watering slightly. Allow soil to dry between waterings. Prefers normal to cool temperatures and high to average humidity. Decrease watering as flowers fade, and let the soil dry out once the cycle is complete. Allow the bulb to remain dormant for at least eight weeks before forcing again.

Cigar Flower
Cuphea ignea

Small, bushy shrub flowers profusely and grows 12–24" (30–60 cm) tall and 8–14" (20–35 cm) wide. Tubular flowers are red and edged purple and cream. They emerge singly from the leaf axils from early summer to late fall. The tiny leaves are widely spaced along wiry stems.

Grow in bright light with some direct sunlight in a well-drained soil-based mix. Keep evenly moist; water less in winter. Prefers higher humidity, normal room temperatures and a minimum winter temperature of 50° F/10° C. Avoid cool, drafty locations. Cut stems back by 2/3 in late winter to keep plant tidy and to encourage flowering for the next year. Repot in spring if necessary. Propagate by taking 2–3" (5.1–7.6 cm) long cuttings in summer or early fall. Sow seed in early spring.

Coffee Plant
Coffea arabica

Bushy tree with glossy, dark green, deeply veined foliage and wavy edges. It can grow 6' (180 cm) tall and produces starry, scented, white flowers in ideal conditions. The leaves and flowers are carried on woody stems. Berries that contain coffee beans may follow the flowers; they are edible but poisonous unless properly roasted before use. 'Nana' is a more compact form.

Coffee plant prefers bright light. Avoid direct sunlight. Keep the soil-based mix moist at all times throughout the year. Average to high humidity and normal room temperatures are best, with a minimum winter temperature of 55°F/13°C. Repot and propagate with cuttings in spring or summer. Prune if necessary to control size and shape.

German Ivy
Delairea odorata

Twining climber, ivy-like plant. The leaves are semi-succulent with pointy lobes carried alternately on thick stems. The stems can reach 24–36" (60–90 cm) lengths. Tiny, scented, yellow flowers may emerge in small clusters but rarely indoors.

German ivy prefers bright light with short periods of direct sunlight. Keep the soil-based potting mix moist at all times, but water less in winter. Average to high humidity and average warmth are best, with a minimum winter temperature of 50°F /10°C. Repot about every two years in spring and propagate by stem cuttings. Often grown in hanging baskets where its trailing habit is best displayed.

Gloxinia
Sinningia speciosa
Bushy plant with large, velvety leaves and trumpet-shaped flowers in a range of colors. Cultivars are more available than the species. Flowers can be solid or bicolored and have ruffled edges and double forms. Most varieties grow no taller than 10–12" (25–30 cm).

Prefers bright light with no direct sunlight. Keep the soil-less mix consistently moist, and don't overwater to prevent rot. High humidity is imperative, so use pebble trays. Average warmth is best, with a minimum winter temperature of 60°F/15°C. Gloxinia is often thrown out after it flowers. To keep it growing, water sparingly until the leaves die, and let the soil dry out. Store the dry tuber in its pot until spring, and repot it hollow side up with fresh mix in spring.

Gold Dust Tree
Aucuba japonica 'Crotonifolia'
Bushy, shrub-like plant with woody stems and large, glossy, oval leaves.

May bear purplish flowers in spring, but sporadically. Bright red berries follow if female and male plants are grown together. 'Crotonifolia' is female with brightly colored foliage and an upright form that can grow up to 36" (90 cm) tall and 24" (60 cm) wide.

Grows well in bright light or partial shade; tolerates direct sunlight only in winter. Keep the soil-based mix moist during the growing season, but allow it to dry slightly between waterings in winter. Prefers high humidity and average warmth, but a cool 50°–60°F/ 10°–15°C in winter. Repot in spring and propagate by seed or stem cuttings late in summer. Cut back older plants at least ⅓ in early spring if too straggly or large.

Madagascar Palm
Pachypodium lamerei
Upright, tree-like succulent with a thick, grayish green stem covered in hard, sharp spines. The leaves emerge from the tip and are narrow, long and shiny. The overall form resembles an open umbrella with a spiky handle. It can grow 7' (3 m) tall but takes a very long time to reach its mature size.

Plants 4' (1.2 m) or taller may produce white, star-shaped flowers in ideal conditions.

Requires bright light but tolerates lower light levels for short periods. Keep the soil-less mix on the dry side but thoroughly soak the soil when watering. It prefers average humidity and normal to cool temperatures. Repot when necessary in spring and propagate by seed.

Rat's-Tail Cactus
Aporocactus flagelliformis
The cylindrical, trailing, fleshy stems of this plant can grow over 36" (90 cm) long and are covered from tip to base in fine, prickly spines. Stems grow densely from the base. Large, multi-layered, bright pink, trumpet-shaped flowers emerge in spring. This plant is often grown in a hanging basket or a heavy container to support the weighty stems. Place in an area away from foot traffic because the fine prickles are difficult to remove from skin or fabric.

Rat's-tail cactus prefers bright sunlight. Water the well-drained, sandy, soil-based potting mix thoroughly, and allow it to dry between waterings. Water less immediately after flowering during its rest period. Low humidity is fine and average warmth is best, with winter temperatures of 45°–50°F/7°–10°C.

Sensitive Plant
Mimosa pudica
Small, bushy shrub that produces feathery leaves made up of tiny, narrow leaflets on wiry stems. Pink, pompom-like flowers emerge from the central stems in summer. It can reach 24" (60 cm) heights but will take an extraordinarily long time to reach its mature size. The foliage is sensitive to touch, movement and temperature.

Sensitive plant prefers bright light with a little direct sunlight. Keep the soil-based consistently mix moist. It prefers average to high humidity and warm temperatures, with a minimum of 15°C/60°F in winter. Propagate with stem cuttings or seed in spring or summer. Repot only if rootbound.

Strawberry Begonia
Saxifraga stolonifera
A rosette of leaves covered in fine hairs and silvery veins. The leaves have scalloped edges and red-flushed undersides. Flowering stems can reach 16" (40 cm), their tiny, white, star-shaped flowers perched high above the foliage. The plant grows to 8" (20 cm), but stolons can trail to 24" (60 cm). 'Tricolor,' a more delicate variety, has variegated green and red or pink leaves with silver or white markings and red undersides.

Requires bright filtered light; 'Tricolor' needs some direct sunlight. Keep the soil-based mix moist but allow it to dry slightly between waterings and water sparingly in winter. Prefers increased humidity, but do not mist. Cool temperatures are best, from 50°–60°F/10°–16°C, with a winter minimum of 45°F/7°C. Keep well ventilated but out of drafts. Propagate by pegging the plantlets down into another container. Repot in spring if necessary.

Swiss Cheese Plant
Monstera deliciosa
Large, sprawling foliar plant with broad, deeply cut leaves and stems covered in thick, fleshy aerial roots. Leaves emerge whole but become deeply cut over time. It can grow to 10' (3 m) if allowed to climb on a moistened moss pole. The aerial roots will grow directly into the moss pole to provide additional support.

Swiss cheese plant prefers moderate light and a soil-based mix. Water moderately throughout the growing season but less in winter. Average humidity and warmth are best, with a minimum winter temperature of 10°C/50°F. Propagate by small tip cuttings or air layering, and repot in spring when necessary.

Vinca
Vinca major 'Wojo's Gem'
Trailing plant with lush foliage on wiry, twining, pale yellow stems. Leaves are variegated creamy yellow and dark green. Violet-blue flowers offset the bright foliage and stems, which can reach 24" (60 cm) lengths or more.

Vinca prefers bright light with periods of direct sunlight. Keep the soil-based mix consistently moist, but allow it to dry slightly between waterings in winter. Average humidity and temperatures are preferable, with a minimum winter temperature of 50°F/10°C. Repot when necessary in spring and propagate with tip cuttings. Grow in a hanging basket to best display the trailing growth, showy foliage and flowers.

Quick Reference Chart

SPECIES by Common Name	Bright	Moderate	Partial Shade	Shade	Direct/Indirect	Filtered	Soil-based	Soil-less	Form	Flowers	Foliage	Fruit/Seed	Scent	Specimen	Grouping
Aeonium	•						•		•		•			•	
African Violet	•				•			•		•	•				•
Aloe	•				•		•		•		•			•	
Angel Wings	•	•			•			•			•			•	
Arrowhead Vine	•		•				•	•	•		•			•	
Asparagus Fern	•					•	•		•		•			•	
Baby's Tears	•					•	•		•		•			•	
Begonia	•	•				•	•	•		•	•			•	
Bridal Veil	•				•		•								
Bromeliad	•				•	•		•	•	•	•			•	
Buddhist Pine	•		•			•	•	•	•		•			•	
Cacti/Succulents	•				•			•	•	•	•				•
Calamondin	•				•			•		•		•		•	•
Calathea			•				•	•			•			•	•
Cardboard Palm	•		•				•		•		•			•	
Cast Iron Plant	•			•			•		•		•			•	•
Century Plant	•						•		•		•			•	
China Doll	•							•							•
Chinese Evergreen	•		•					•			•				•
Clog Plant	•		•	•				•	•	•	•			•	
Coleus	•				•		•				•			•	•
Croton	•				•		•		•		•			•	•
Crown of Thorns	•						•		•	•				•	
Cyclamen	•	•					•			•	•				•
Devil's Ivy	•	•		•				•	•		•			•	•
Dracaena	•	•		•				•	•		•			•	
Dumb Cane	•	•					•	•			•			•	
Elephant's Ear	•		•				•		•		•			•	

SOIL CONDITION						FORM				HUMIDITY			Page Number	SPECIES by Common Name
Moist	Well-drained	Dry	Fertile	Average	Poor	Upright	Bushy	Climber/Trailer	Architectural	Low	Average	High		
•	•		•			•			•		•		62	Aeonium
•	•		•			•						•	64	African Violet
	•	•	•			•			•		•		68	Aloe
•	•		•			•	•				•		70	Angel Wings
•	•		•				•	•				•	72	Arrowhead Vine
•				•			•	•			•	•	74	Asparagus Fern
•				•				•				•	76	Baby's Tears
•		•		•			•	•				•	78	Begonia
•				•			•	•			•	•	82	Bridal Veil
•	•			•		•	•		•		•	•	84	Bromeliad
•		•		•		•	•		•		•	•	88	Buddhist Pine
•	•	•		•	•	•	•	•	•	•	•	•	90	Cacti/Succulents
•		•		•		•	•				•	•	96	Calamondin
•				•		•	•					•	98	Calathea
•	•				•	•			•		•	•	100	Cardboard Palm
	•	•			•	•			•	•			102	Cast Iron Plant
	•	•		•		•			•	•	•		104	Century Plant
•				•		•	•				•	•	106	China Doll
•				•		•	•					•	108	Chinese Evergreen
•				•			•	•				•	110	Clog Plant
•				•			•				•		112	Coleus
•	•		•			•	•				•	•	114	Croton
•	•				•	•			•	•			116	Crown of Thorns
•		•	•				•				•	•	118	Cyclamen
•					•	•	•	•			•	•	120	Devil's Ivy
•	•				•	•	•		•		•		122	Dracaena
•				•		•	•		•		•	•	128	Dumb Cane
•				•		•			•		•	•	130	Elephant's Ear

SPECIES
by Common Name

SPECIES by Common Name	LIGHT						SOIL MIX		FEATURES						
	Bright	Moderate	Partial Shade	Shade	Direct/Indirect	Filtered	Soil-based	Soil-less	Form	Flowers	Foliage	Fruit/Seed	Scent	Specimen	Grouping
English Ivy		•	•		•			•	•		•			•	•
False Aralia	•						•		•		•			•	•
Ferns	•	•					•		•		•			•	•
Ficus	•		•				•	•	•		•	•		•	•
Flamingo Flower	•				•			•		•	•				•
Flowering Maple	•				•			•		•				•	•
Gardenia	•							•		•			•		•
Grape Ivy		•					•	•	•		•			•	
Jade Plant	•							•	•	•	•			•	•
Japanese Sago Palm	•				•		•	•	•		•			•	
Jasmine	•	•			•		•				•		•		•
Kalanchoe	•				•		•			•	•				•
Leaf Flower	•					•	•	•			•				•
Lipstick Plant	•				•			•	•	•	•			•	
Lucky Bean	•				•		•				•			•	
Ming Aralia	•		•		•		•		•		•			•	•
Monkey Plant	•				•		•				•	•			•
Norfolk Island Pine	•				•		•		•		•			•	•
Orchids	•	•					•	•		•				•	
Ornamental Pepper	•				•			•				•			•
Paper Flower	•				•		•		•	•				•	
Parlor Palm	•	•					•		•		•			•	•
Passion Flower	•				•		•		•	•	•			•	•
Peace Lily		•	•					•	•	•	•			•	•
Peperomia	•	•						•	•	•	•			•	•
Philodendron	•	•					•				•			•	•
Piggyback Plant	•				•	•	•	•	•		•			•	•
Pilea	•	•			•			•	•		•				•

SOIL CONDITION						FORM				HUMIDITY			Page Number	SPECIES by Common Name
Moist	Well-drained	Dry	Fertile	Average	Poor	Upright	Bushy	Climber/Trailer	Architectural	Low	Average	High		
•			•				•	•			•	•	132	English Ivy
•	•			•			•	•	•		•	•	134	False Aralia
•	•		•	•			•	•			•	•	136	Ferns
•	•			•	•	•	•	•	•		•	•	142	Ficus
•	•		•				•				•	•	146	Flamingo Flower
	•	•		•		•	•				•		148	Flowering Maple
•			•				•					•	150	Gardenia
•				•			•	•			•		152	Grape Ivy
	•	•			•		•		•	•	•		154	Jade Plant
	•	•		•	•				•	•	•		156	Japanese Sago Palm
•				•				•			•	•	158	Jasmine
•	•			•			•				•		160	Kalanchoe
•				•			•					•	164	Leaf Flower
	•	•	•					•				•	166	Lipstick Plant
•	•				•	•			•		•		168	Lucky Bean
•	•			•	•	•	•		•		•	•	170	Ming Aralia
•				•			•	•			•	•	172	Monkey Plant
•					•	•	•		•		•		174	Norfolk Island Pine
•	•			•			•					•	176	Orchids
•				•			•					•	180	Ornamental Pepper
•				•				•	•		•		182	Paper Flower
•				•		•	•					•	184	Parlor Palm
•			•					•	•		•	•	186	Passion Flower
•					•		•		•		•	•	188	Peace Lily
•	•			•	•		•	•				•	190	Peperomia
•				•			•	•	•	•		•	194	Philodendron
•				•			•	•			•	•	198	Piggyback Plant
		•		•			•	•				•	200	Pilea

SPECIES
by Common Name

SPECIES by Common Name	LIGHT						SOIL MIX		FEATURES						
	Bright	Moderate	Partial Shade	Shade	Direct/Indirect	Filtered	Soil-based	Soil-less	Form	Flowers	Foliage	Fruit/Seed	Scent	Specimen	Grouping
Plush Vine	•				•		•		•		•			•	
Polka Dot Plant	•				•	•		•			•				•
Ponytail Palm	•				•		•		•		•			•	
Prayer Plant	•	•				•	•				•			•	•
Rosary Vine	•				•		•		•	•	•	•		•	
Rose of China	•				•		•		•	•	•			•	•
Silk Oak	•		•			•	•		•		•			•	•
Silver Vine	•	•			•		•		•		•				•
Silvery Inch Plant	•		•				•	•	•		•			•	
Snake Plant	•		•				•		•		•			•	
Spider Plant	•	•						•	•		•			•	
Spineless Yucca	•				•		•		•		•			•	
Spreading Clubmoss			•	•				•	•		•			•	•
String of Beads	•				•		•		•		•			•	
Swedish Ivy	•		•					•	•		•			•	
Umbrella Tree	•	•						•	•		•			•	
Velvet Plant	•				•		•	•	•		•			•	
Wandering Jew	•				•		•		•		•			•	
Wax Plant	•				•			•	•		•			•	•
ZZ Plant	•		•			•	•		•		•			•	•

| SOIL CONDITION | | | | | | FORM | | | | HUMIDITY | | | | SPECIES by Common Name |
Moist	Well-drained	Dry	Fertile	Average	Poor	Upright	Bushy	Climber/Trailer	Architectural	Low	Average	High	Page Number	
•				•		•	•				•		204	Plush Vine
•				•			•				•		206	Polka Dot Plant
	•	•			•				•			•	208	Ponytail Palm
•			•				•					•	210	Prayer Plant
•	•				•			•	•	•			212	Rosary Vine
•	•			•			•				•	•	214	Rose of China
•	•			•		•	•					•	216	Silk Oak
•				•					•			•	218	Silver Vine
•				•					•		•		220	Silvery Inch Plant
•					•	•			•	•			222	Snake Plant
•				•			•	•	•		•		224	Spider Plant
•					•	•			•	•			226	Spineless Yucca
•					•		•				•	•	228	Spreading Clubmoss
•	•				•			•	•	•			230	String of Beads
•					•		•				•		232	Swedish Ivy
•				•		•	•		•		•		234	Umbrella Tree
•				•			•					•	236	Velvet Plant
•	•				•	•	•				•		238	Wandering Jew
	•	•			•			•	•		•		240	Wax Plant
	•	•			•			•	•		•		242	ZZ Plant

Glossary

Acid – potting mix or medium that contains little or no lime, with a pH lower than 7.

Alkaline – potting mix or medium that usually contains lime, with a pH above 7.

Anther – the pollen-bearing portion of a flower, on the upper section of the stamen.

Axil – the angle between the stem and the leafstalk that emerges from it.

Bract – a modified leaf, usually brightly colored and found at the base of the flower. It can be large or small and is often mistaken for a petal or the flower itself.

Calyx – the group or collective outer covering of a flower bud, made up of modified leaves or sepals.

Chelated iron – a complex chemical additive containing iron or other metal form used to treat and prevent chlorosis, typically caused by an iron or magnesium deficiency. It also helps plants to better absorb nutrients.

Chlorosis or Chlorotic – yellowing leaves, often caused by a nutrient deficiency.

Complete fertilizer - a fertilizer that supplies some of all three major nutrients; proportions may vary from one fertilizer to the next. It is different from a simple fertilizer that contains only one plant nutrient.

Corona – a crown-like structure, sometimes on the corolla or petals of a flower.

Crown – the area of a plant where the stem and roots meet, often at soil level, or the top portion of a tree or shrub, above the level of the lowest branch.

Cultivar – a variety that has been bred in cultivation rather than naturally occurring in the wild.

Dormant – a temporary period of inactivity, usually when top growth and roots die back, as opposed to a rest period, when plants produce little or no growth but retain their foliage.

Epiphyte – a plant that grows upon or attaches itself to another plant, rather than growing in from the ground in soil. The plant absorbs nutrients and water through aerial roots, from the air and available precipitation.

F1 Hybrid – a first generation offspring of two plants of closely related or purebred strains. F1 hybrids are often more vigorous than an ordinary hybrid or either parent and have more desirable qualities. F1 hybrids produce seeds that rarely produce plants of comparable value, however.

Filaments – a slender supportive stalk that carries the pollen-bearing anther.

Frond – the leaf-like part of a fern or the leaf of a palm.

Genus – a group of related species.

Habit – the general shape and form of a plant, e.g., bushy, spreading, upright.

Humus – rotted organic matter in the soil that improves soil structure.

Hybrid – a plant resulting from a cross between two unidentical parents.

Leaflet – a single segment of a divided leaf.

Microclimate – environmental or atmospheric conditions in a small area different from those of the surrounding area.

Midrib – the central vein or rib, generally raised, on the underside of a leaf or leaflet.

Monopodial – an orchid that produces a single stem from the roots at the base.

Node – the part of a plant where the stem meets the leaf.

Organic – any material derived from a living source, such as plants and animals.

Organic fertilizer – an animal or plant product or by-product used as fertilizer. Usually mineral based and naturally produced.

Organic gardening – a process of growing plants without the use of synthetic fertilizers or pesticides.

Organic pesticide – a pesticide derived from natural sources and made with minimal processing.

Potting mix or medium – a growing mixture specially prepared for plants grown in pots.

Pseudobulb – a thickened or swollen stem, often the base of many orchid species, which stores the water and food that the plant will live from during the dry season. The leaves also emerge from this stem.

Rhizome – a fleshy or swollen, horizontal stem that both roots and shoots emerge from.

Semi-terrestrial – an orchid that grows in leaf litter and humus on top of a fast-draining substrate, such as rock.

Sepal – a modified leaf, arranged in a ring outside the petals, which covers the flower bud. A group of sepals make up the calyx.

Spadix – a fleshy flower spike bearing tiny embedded florets. The spadix is usually enclosed in a leaf-like spathe. The spadix is sometimes the color of the spathe or a contrasting color.

Spathe – a leaf-like bract, sometimes white or brightly colored, which encloses a flower cluster or spadix. The peace lily, flamingo flower and Chinese evergreen flowers have spathes.

Stamen – the male reproductive parts of a flower, including the pollen-producing anther and the filament that supports the anther.

Stems – the structure or frame that carries the leaves and flowers. Stems can take many forms, from the trunk of a tree to the trailing runners of a vine to the branches of a shrub.

Stigma – the tip of the female portion of the flower or pistil on which pollen is deposited from the male.

Sympodial – orchids that have many stems arising from a horizontal stem.

Synthetic fertilizer – a fertilizer produced through chemical manipulation of raw materials as opposed to naturally occurring substances.

Synthetic pesticide – a pesticide synthesized from petroleum-derived materials.

Tendril – a thin, thread-like modified stem that coils around or grabs onto anything surrounding it.

Terrestrial – an orchid or bromeliad that grows in the ground or in soil.

Index of plant names

Entries in **bold** type indicate the main plant headings.